MY IRELAND
MY ENGLAND

MY IRELAND
MY ENGLAND

An Amazing Life
An Astounding Solution

Paddy McGarvey

Copyright © 2012 by Paddy McGarvey.

ISBN: Softcover   978-1-4797-2850-3
           Ebook   978-1-4797-2851-0

All rights reserved. No part of this book may be reproduced or transmitted in any form or by any means, electronic or mechanical, including photocopying, recording, or by any information storage and retrieval system, without permission in writing from the copyright owner.

This book was printed in the United States of America.

Rev. date: 08/18/2013

To order additional copies of this book, contact:
Xlibris Corporation
0-800-644-6988
www.Xlibrispublishing.co.uk
Orders@Xlibrispublishing.co.uk

CONTENTS

Chapter One	I Arrive—Luckily and Pluckily	19
Chapter Two	The Boy Steps Out or to Macroom and Back	23
Chapter Three	Big City Newsman. 1947	41
Chapter Four	To England—Dear Sam	52
Chapter Five	Sussex by the Sea	58
Chapter Six	1954 The Sunday Dispatch	70
Chapter Seven	In Paris With Gina	81
Chapter Eight	A Mirror to Ireland.	92
Chapter Nine	A Bad Confession	102
Chapter Ten	Campaigning in Ulster	111
Chapter Eleven	1964 More Mid Ulster	118
Chapter Twelve	The truant MPs	130
Chapter Thirteen	The Tale of Trilby	138
Chapter Fourteen	1984 A Cabinet Minister On Ice	144
Chapter Fifteen	My One Day at Balliol	151
Chapter Sixteen	Averill Lukic Intervenes	157
Chapter Seventeen	Just Some More Bits	164

Epilogue 171

The author in his early motoring days—the private hand built 1930 Plywood-frame Gran Tourismo sedan with rotary pedal transmission and back-pedal brakes. Note the bold questing glance of the future Fleet Street star (shooting)

For Nuala

Remembering Jimmy

United States Department of State

Washington, D.C. 20520

October 11, 1995

Mr. Paddy McGarvey
Irish Parliament Trust
Rainbow Building
Armagh, Northern Ireland
BT61 7BN
United Kingdom

Dear Mr. McGarvey:

    Your letter to President Clinton of September 19, 1995 discussing the objectives of the Irish Parliament Trust has been referred to this office for reply.

    The idea of a neutral parliament center for the island of Ireland is one that we have not encountered before. It certainly provokes thought and your comparison to other countries which chose a neutral location for their capital, including the United States, is interesting. I will undertake to circulate the ideas and information that you provided to those offices within the U.S. government most concerned with the peace process in Northern Ireland.

    The President will visit the leaders of both governments, as well as the people of Northern Ireland at the end of November. We expect his visit will underscore the support of the United States for the joint efforts of the British and Irish governments and the people of Northern Ireland to achieve a lasting and peaceful settlement.

    Thank you for sharing your ideas and concerns for a peaceful resolution to the conflict in Northern Ireland. We continue to hope that all parties will be flexible and creative in the search for peace.

Sincerely,

Paul B. van Son
Officer-in-Charge
Ireland/Northern Ireland Affairs

A letter to the Trust, then in Armagh, (but not now) from the US State Department in 1995 reveals to the author and others their interest in his astounding solution. It was actually one they had pioneered themselves, for America, over 200 years ago, and which other former colonies have successfully copied.

    McGarvey says here that Ireland still needs a shared capital with an unhindered franchise for all.

PROLOGUE—MINUS TWO

In 1948, an ambitious 20 year-old Irish journalist with law and law-reporting experience, arrived in Shrewsbury at 9.15 a.m to join a national press agency, tired and hungry after the night boat from Dublin, two trains, and a six hour wait at Crewe Junction. His new boss shook hands in the office at Shoplatch and sent him back up the town to a divorce court. He bought himself a Mars bar for breakfast. After an hour of taking down the most lubricious evidence he had ever heard, about women's underwear draped over a chair, a man in her bed and his shoes under it, the court rose, the clerk sent the bailiff out for a policeman who took him downstairs to a cell. The constable shut the door.

The clerk arrived and offered the prisoner a cigarette, declined. He took off his wig and sat down beside him to ask who he was, who he worked for, where did he come from, and when? The reporter replied—Paddy McGarvey, Bryce Thomas Press Agency in Shoplatch, from Dublin, this morning, and the clerk roared with laughter

"You are not allowed to write down evidence in divorce; it is illegal. You should have been told that by your editor. You must wait to hear the judge's summary and decision, to report that if you wish." Resuming his wig, he told the police there would be no charge, and to release him. The clerk told the resumed court he comes only this very this morning from a country which forbids divorce, and the court roared with laughter. His meekly polite employer, Leslie Bryce Thomas, arrived and took him back to the office, on this, his first morning, job, court, day, police cell, in England.

PROLOGUE—MINUS ONE

August 1949, now 21, undaunted, he responded from Dublin to a telegram from the Sussex Express, Lewes, to cover the trial of the century that would send the acid-bath killer John George Haigh to the gallows. At Lewes railway station, newly nationalised British Railways lost all his luggage and travel papers. Window shopping High Street an hour before the trial to replace his festering underwear and corroding socks in the heatwave of the century, he was unaware that the Editor of the Daily Mirror had gone to goal for contempt of the trial, while reading the amazing safety headline by the Daily Express—

IRA Gun Gang to Murder Judge.
MI5 guard Lewes Assizes.

He grinned at that ridiculous story just as two men emerged from a bottle-green Wolesely saloon with Lion and Unicorn emblems on the doors. Who are you, where do you come from, what are you doing here, and why are you walking up and down the street? He answered, Paddy McGarvey, Dublin, a reporter on the Sussex Express, and I am attending the Haigh trial. They asked again—Passport, sailing ticket, when did you join the paper, and what is the editor's name? To which he replied, lost by BR, ditto, this morning, William Shakespeare. As they elbowed him through the double-doors of the police station he brushed shoulders with a thick-set man in a heavy overcoat, the cold-blooded Haigh on the way to his trial. He was placed in a cell, the door shut. The editor was assisting police at Hastings seaside after a burglary at his wife's fish and chip shop, which had no phone. The paper's managing director, George Martin responded: "McGarvey, Dublin you say? A most unlikely story, especially the telegram. We would never do that" A sheepish Ralph Ravenshear aka "William Shakespeare" arrived at noon and took him to the office. He never saw Haigh again. Second trip to England, second job, first day, in an English police cell for three hours.

Then, only months into his third job in England, came this . . .

PROLOGUE

A KING EMPEROR, HIS CASTLE AND HIS QUEENS

The King, the Queen and their younger Princess emerged from a castle corner. They were unaccompanied, no guards or servants. There was no ceremony, no salute. This was their home after all, and their resemblance to an ordinary upper crust family emerging after lunch for a day out was striking. Michael Wagen, a grand-sibling of Jewish immigrants driven from their homes by the King's kinsman, the Czar of all the Russias, turned to the Irishman waiting beside him and murmured: "Ready Paddy?" Mesmerised, I was ready . . .

> The Jew and the Catholic stood quite still as the Royal three drew near.

The converted orange-box strapped to my complaining left shoulder was ticking and clicking with glowing lights. I moved closer to Mike so as not to foul the connection as he took aim. As photographer and reporter we were linked by a trailing electric wire as together we faced the anointed Head of the English Protestant Church, the Emperor of India, King by the Grace of God of Great Britain and Northern Ireland, her Dominions, Colonies, Protectorates and Territories Overseas. A recent immigrant from the unhappy Irish fringe of his Kingdom, I was nervously over-awed at such intimacy, so soon if ever at all, alongside by mere inches the living symbol of my country's oppression. The boys at the Protestant end of Armagh, would spit blood if they could see me now. *What, that wee Fenian skitter with our King in his* castle For three months now the boy wonder had survived England without another police cell and now this was happening.

There was no one to get in our way, not a single sentry, no police presence, no watchful snipers on the castle battlements, spy helicopters barely invented.

To our right stood three lines of elderly civilians mostly in wide short trousers under wide-brim hats, while many of them in kilts displayed daggers peeping from the top of their thick woollen socks. At the Town

Gate outside, a burly Bobby with a "wingco" moustache gave a cursory dekko at my box and grinned: "Refreshments, sir?" as he showed us in.

Mike raised the chrome sight of the big American Speed Graphic camera and began shooting as King George VI reached the front line of Scoutmasters leading the World Jamboree encamped in the Royal Great Park stretching away from the castle. This quiet gathering inside it was compromise to a cancelled inspection of hundreds of scouts outside for which the King was not quite fit. By now Mike and I, still wired, and backing away from the advancing King, noticed that he was wearing hinged shoes. The toecaps of his laced Oxfords slid back and forward overlapping the uppers as he walked. There was no sign of a limp.

The early morning of April 23rd 1950 had been overcast and wet. The rain had eased by noon, but the gloom from grey skies persisted all day, a low daylight boxed in here by the high grey walls around us, and the reason I was carrying the world's first photo-flash accumulator. The early versions were modified from the orange boxes post-war tenants and squatters were using as furniture; ten years later the accumulators were thimble-sized inside Japanese cameras. The huge box wrenching down my left shoulder was meant to relieve the photographer from rapid changes of flash bulbs.

The size of the castle was another thing. It left me in architectural awe. I had seen it for the first time only weeks before, ambling along Eton High Street until a gentle dog-leg kink in the street suddenly opens the view to William the Conqueror's Great Keep towering over the Thames. Any political or social measurement I had of castles in Ireland vanished in a second, rocking my inner Irish animosity to things British. Why fight a people who could build this? Mike Wagen and I were wired together for life on that day, until the sad day he died fifty years later. The King had barely two years to live.

King George's plain mufti emphasised his sallow complexion, but his gaze was hawk-like and alert to his surroundings, most noticeably the questioning nod and narrowed eyebrows he gave to my big box. The body language indicated his wondering what I was carrying around. A slight grimace accompanied his questing eye; for a second or two I thought he was going to ask, and Mike looked round anxiously. He was concentrating on the daughter He told me later he thought *I was going to say something.*

Princess Margaret was the darling of Haut *Mayfair*. Emerging from that hidden doorway she had not quite got her cigarette holder back into her handbag and Mike was kicking himself for missing this vital evidence of her "habit". Had the smoking Princess just stomped out a butt? What a scoop that would have been, only to be shared by the local press outside for whom we were "pooling". On our way back to the office I jested about my own antecedents, trying to explain what it meant to an aspirant Irishman seeking a place in the world, and there I was, begob, with the King of England's Daughter already, the Irishman's dream on his first migrating walk. No one in any kind of authority had queried who Mike and I were, or where we came from, when it was the Slough Observer's turn to take the royal press pool. In 1950, *Security* was a word which referred to insurance policies, and; "tight security" was a cliché yet unborn.

Britain slumbered in an inertia of post-war peace even as the Korean war involving her soldiers yet again, would soon rage on the other side of the planet A big sergeant from the Gaelic side of Ireland with the un-Gaelic name Bill Speakman won the VC with the 'Glorious Gloucesters.' Brendan Behan, once a would-be boy terrorist for Ireland, languished profitably in a Borstal gaol, the governor taking a interest in his change of outlook. Later in that brief career he wrote a column for an English Sunday paper, The People, which I had to vet at times, but for an overuse of liquid indulgence in the text. The Anglo-Irish paradoxes continued. It was as if the 'Thirties had returned intact, but with full employment, alongside overcrowded housing, free doctors, secondary schools and hospitals. The papers were still four-page skinny. Food was frugal and as limited in choice as scarcity decreed. Petrol was rationed. You needed coupons for clothes, but the loitering Teddy Boys managed to create a unique working-class style out of a frock coat cut square to the knee, a stringy black tie, a pair of trousers and deep foam-rubber platform shoes.

As the mid-century turned on itself, the seminal changes of Suez, rock and roll, the IRA skirmishing again in Ulster, and then the Beatles, were waiting in the wings to batter the country into the more salivating Sixties.

Beginning early in the war, every August, between Windsor Castle and *Slough the Home of Horlicks* (as the station name-boards had it) only two miles away, the local commoners took over the sacrosanct playing fields of Eton for home-based carnival entertainments. A Fur and Feather Show, for pets, took pride of place alongside The *Best Head of Hair Competition* for their owners, the prizes for which encouraged good hygiene amid the travails of war. In the early 'Fifties the week-long carnival, begun as a war emergency to persuade people to holiday at home, petered out in whiffs of financial scandal, and the college retreated unscathed behind cloister and walls. I joined The Slough Observer to undergo a tempestuous conditioning for Fleet Street by a gimlet-eyed editor, and to meet the mother of my six children, as well as adopting the one she made earlier with her first husband, a Serbian soldier in the exiled court of King Peter of Yugoslavia, by then in America to become Director of Slav Studies in Pittsburgh University.

The King died at Sandringham, his private Norfolk home, 18 months later. I was sitting in Windsor County Court, a regular Wednesday mark in the newsroom diary. Harry the Bailiff came bustling in, strode to the clerk's desk, and stretched himself up beyond him to whisper hoarsely to Judge H.C. Leon that the King was dead. We all heard him. The judge adjourned the court for an hour "to allow us to collect our thoughts at this very sad news."

The court's remit area for the local press embraced Slough and south Bucks, to the north of the Thames. It was an important source of news for the Slough Observer, this judge in particular making national headlines from seemingly mundane casework. Judge Harry Leon's initials, H.C, concealed the author of successful novels spoofing the law and lawyers, Henry Cecil. Of several which made it to the cinema screen, Brothers in Law, starring Ian Carmichael, comes easiest to mind, the book and the film I enjoyed, unaware I had been sitting in the author's weekly court for four years. I walked out into Peascod Street to look up at the Castle. There was no flag on the Keep. The dead king was in Norfolk and the new monarch, his daughter Elizabeth, was proclaimed Queen while visiting an elaborate tree-house in Kenya. On the day in November 1949 I was interviewed for this job, I arrived too early from Sussex and took time to look at the town centre, Slough Crown. The largest car I had ever seen pulled up at the traffic lights; only three feet away from me, Princess Elizabeth gave me a brief nodding smile before turning to her lady-in-waiting alongside her under the Rolls Royce Landau's huge glass display hood. The lights turned and the Rolls glided silently around them—in other countries it could have done that on the red light—to take the last lap from Buckingham Palace to Windsor, the only direct road route at the time. The Observer sent its Irish Catholic reporter over to Windsor again to describe and explain in solemn words to its readers, their king's funeral. It was the choice by wordsmith, not for my religion; such thinking did not exist in the English regional press.

This time I was just outside the castle. There is a lamppost on the greensward near the George 1V Gate It is singular, standing alone in corpulent abutments and scrolls under glittering black paint and gilt. I had the bottom ledge, one buttock supported by one arm around the post, my other leg dangling. Improbable now to imagine, there were two German journalists on another ledge above mine. Years away in my future I would turn to the legends of that king's father," Farmer" George III, (1760-1820) in an attempt to link his mishandling of the American colony with what was happening still in Ireland. He was a devout Anglican, and unusually for a British monarch until recent times, a faithful husband; the playwright Alan Bennett has them conversing in their bedroom as "Mr. King" and "Mrs. King". However mild-mannered before and after the mysterious illness that smote him twice in his reign, he raged at religious defaulters and dubbed the Ulster Scots taking over and winning the American Revolution, "the wrong kind of Protestants" They were Presbyterians well settled in Ireland since the Elizabethan plantations but felt forced to leave by the Test Acts begun by Queen Anne early in the 18th century—Communicate in my Church of England or you are nothing." The WASPs who founded America were not merely White Anglo Saxon Protestants, as her school-children are taught, but more racially and religiously accurate, White Angry Scottish Presbyterians—from Ireland. Farmer George rode out frequently, just to fuss over his farms, a view that now stretches for a landscaped mile to the Copper Horse statue, interrupted only by the county road to Old Windsor and London's more salubrious south-west suburbs. The royal bier came from London by train to Windsor GWR station, and from there, here, up this rising path to the castle's side-gate. The whole world's regal and powerful, elected, anointed, or usurping, would reveal themselves as rarely before or after.

Minor Asian emperors, Europe's quieter kings, presidents and prime ministers, dazzling South American dictators, splendid sultans, all climbed the long hill to the gate in solemn tread, taking this king-emperor back to his castle for the last time. All were yards apart, three by three, a paradise for aspiring assassins. The greatest visible drama came, not from exotic emperors in white and gold & finery, but from the three Windsor women in solemn plain black garb, comforting each other in one plain black carriage pulled by a single Irish dray. There were three lawful queens of England in this unique fragment of its history, his daughter, his widow, and his mother. It was matched, some would have argued, only by the four royal dukes walking separately abreast behind, Edinburgh, Kent, Gloucester and yes, Windsor, the king who never quite was, a 20th century cameo from a 17th century drama at The Globe. "Look" cried one of the Germans further up my pole: "there's Adenauer. He is bent over. He is finished. He will be next." Journalists' predictions! Konrad Adenauer, prime minister of West

Germany, did indeed look pale and frail, but he was far from "next". In the 13 years left to his elected rule, he brought warmth and reconciliation to vanquished and victors.

A more familiar scene soon appeared, two mourners walking shoulder to shoulder, talking to each other "two to the dozen" as we say, black Ulster overcoats open and flapping, Anthony Eden hats set back on their heads, surely two Irishmen with the habits of home, where a funeral march is a talk fest. It was soon easy to recognise Taoiseach—Prime Minister—Eamon DeValera, and his Foreign Secretary, Frank Aiken. Their very presence here gave me a momentary frisson of mirth. Aiken was said to have been Dev's favourite gunman. He couldn't abide the things himself.

Dev was reputed by some to have lain flat on the top floor (such as where I might have been myself) of Boland's Mill throughout as the 1916 Easter rebels took aim at the Sherwood Foresters marching in from the troopships at Kingstown Harbour. Yet Aiken had striven might and main to stop the civil war that Dev started when the 1922 Treaty offering the 26 counties dominion status was approved by the Dail and people. Around that stupid split the Republic votes to this day, mired in its own bitter history, a country split by the Irish-Spaniard's obduracy over two mere words, dominion or republic I wondered now what they were talking about; more than likely, second preferences in the next election. It was no skin off Dev's nose to mourn in person the British monarch. I should have told my pole-sharing Germans that he had called on the German Embassy in Dublin to express condolences on the death of Hitler. It made Churchill apoplectic in his poor-mouth Irish-scorning victory speech. Dev's De Mortuis nil nisi Bonum reply was a fair par for the course, piercing the Churchill rhetoric, but spoiled by the Irish-partition whinge that followed. He's seen them all off. Sure wasn't even poor dead Michael Collins a grand fellow after all, didn't Dev say, eventually, sure to be God!

CHAPTER ONE

I Arrive—Luckily and Pluckily

Barely an hour had passed and my afterbirth discreetly cleared away so that my mother was as comfortable as could be, when Mr. Frank McArdle's gleaming black Austin hackney limousine arrived at the front door of then No. 25 Railway Street, Armagh, to take me to the cathedral for my baptism and Christening. The immediacy of these events, in the early winter of November 1927, was wrought by the high rate of infant mortality prevailing in Ireland at that time. The advent of the new state of Northern Ireland in that same decade had changed nothing in this respect, as with most things in Ireland. The peril lay very close. Of five previous sons born to my parents since their marriage in the severe food-shortage year of 1917, only one had survived birth, my austere and strait-laced brother, James John, on June 13th 1923. I have to describe him thus. I am not being unkind. You see, I was his opposite in all things, beginning as the younger brother, a situation of pertinent cruelty that also provided the country, and the world, with a surfeit of Irish priests. An Irish language scholar, he dubbed me, in the Irish "flahuile" (my phonetic spelling) a reckless spendthrift.

So it was understandable that a black cloud of doubt hung over my very survival. This panic-driven race to the Cathedral should ensure that on my death in infancy I would go straight to join the cherubic angels of paradise via a sanctified grave. Not for me the legion of Limbo babies who would never see God, so my reverend teachers explained from as early as infants's class. The Armagh contingent were dumped in a big meadow of unmarked graves hidden beyond the top of the cemetery hill as it rolled back down towards the Monaghan railway line. I remember thinking, as I became aware of them, that it was nice the lost babies could at least see the choo-trains, which for children who came into the world dead, but children always in the afterlife, was a reasonable exchange for God. Then the line was closed. In the womb they were entitled to life and soul from conception, so say the ruling males of my austere, unyielding church, but arriving dead, they were devoid of souls and discarded like offal. Only when writing this chapter in Cambridge did I learn from a distinguished church historian that earlier in this decade the Pope had summoned a few fathers of the church to his holiday home at Castle Gandolfo to consider and pronounce this cruel edict of Holy Church (!!) wrong, having no origin in anything taught by the Junior Carpenter in the Workshop at Nazareth. If there was any sense in its origin, it can only lie with the holy Doctors who jailed Galilleo for denying that the sun went round the earth. So anyway, I then must have felt safe in the arms of my equally austere grandmother, Mary Ann Mullaly, nee Tyrell, her mother nee Race. She was the widow of a prison warder, to whose religion she had converted when he was a decorated Royal Dublin Fusilier just home from expanding the empire, and she the only child of tolerant farming parents. This was how my warm and motherly Aunt Bazie would explain her mother's origins. "Ach, she came off a Protestant farm near Tullamore"—but would say no more. I suspect her hesitation lay in the fact that Granny had been a Presbyterian, *quelle horreur*, a protestant Protestant, a reverberation still around.

Elizabeth's Irish Wars, ending in her death, left unintended vacancies wide open to the new Scottish king's landless border riff raff of broken clans in the lowlands, and after witnessing James VI of Scotland's great baggage train, reputed five miles long, trundling off to London where he would become James I of both countries, they poured over to a stricken, open, unruly Ulster. Most of the planters stopped at the bleak stretches of sandy soil amid boggy terrain extending westward from Monaghan to Leitrim, which is why most of Ulster is Protestant Ulster today. Admitting to a "Protestant" ancestor in the immediate family was bearable, at least within the family's own confines, the Presbyterian variety, twice reviled everywhere outside Scotland as not to be mentioned, not even in politer Protestant, Church of Ireland, company.

Two hundred yards from our house, later renumbered to 87, Mr. McArdle pulled up at the City Mills in Lower English Street, which later housed the timber and builders yards of McKenna Brothers, to collect the bookkeeper, Miss Alice Murphy. Unmarried Alice was our lodger and had undertaken the duties of Godmother, my turn now. Alice was a dainty doll-like little Monaghan lady of indeterminate age who walked with long springing strides on remarkably high heels, which she liked to think gave her added authority. She was not unknown to take her nice new ones off, passing them around the table at meals for inspection. She came bustling excitedly out to the car with Mick yet shaking her head and tut-tutting in some sense of secondary bewilderment. "How wonderful" she chorused to Granny Mullaly, "another wee boy" while thinking of the four lost boys "but when, Mrs. Mullaly, are we going to get a wee girl? That's what I want to know!" Four years later, on February 6th 1932, Alice got her wish in the form of my sister Nuala. For the arrival of a girl to the long-serving council chairman's wife, bells were rung, mostly on glasses with spoons, Aged four, I was thought old enough to be brought to the birth room to see her. I first laid eyes on my sister under a light steel birth cage supporting the bed clothes, as she lay sleeping between her mother's hip and breast.

The answer from inside the car came from the Presbyterian still inside my Granny. In spite of several trips to Rome to make sure the Pope was up to scratch, interspersed with trips to the States to visit her three sons, Father John Mullaly SJ, Leo the golf pro, and Myles the power-company road man. The answer could only have been an impatient *hummph* to dampen Alice down. There was serious business to hand. Alice would be asked to "name this child" but it was the Granny who was under orders of eviction or worse from my angry father to get it right this time.

And so with Alice aboard, the christening party turned into Cathedral Road and the big car purred up the Car Walk, the easy gradient that circled the steep bluff on which the twin-spired cathedral perched. The twin spires were a compromise to a central tower which was thought to be too heavy for the design. From the middle distance it looked like a rabbit sitting on a football. It was then I like to think, at that early age, not much more than an hour old, I got my taste for big powerful motor cars. After the same fervent rush to the cathedral with my brother four years before, but none for the fourth dead baby in between Jimmy and I, my well-humoured level-headed father, a law clerk of Edwardian weight and principles, not to mention the authority he exercised over the city fathers, returned from a day of briefing a barrister at Sligo Assizes, a fair hundred miles away, to find his first surviving child, a son, named after his late, prison-warder father-in-law, James., who wasn't even around to enjoy that honour. He died in 1911. "Daddy" was Patrick James, thus the familiar "P.J" you find in various leadership roles of many an Irish town. He decreed by way of redemption that I was to be Patrick Joseph, such was the importance of retaining the favoured initials as well as his patrimony. Any hint that his mother-in-law should move out, as she could easily afford, as many a son-in-law might wish, had a serious snag. "Our house," as with several others on both sides of Railway Street, was actually "her house." The irony of this impasse would not have been lost on "P.J." In yet another life of several, he was an amateur concert artist of song and story, indeed deeply loved as something of a star, especially at shows for church-related charities. In the years of commonplace Irish bachelorhood before his marriage at 38, my mother 20, a not uncommon union, he led an amateur quartet of musical companions. Owen "Owney" Webb, was a cork salesman, Peter O'Hare, a clerk o' works (who would father a large family of gifted amateur musicians) and Mickey Mullan, who was a chemist. "Making up the Bill" for the seaside impressarios, they performed only in the Isle of Man at the height of the summer season in Douglas. It was a bachelor-boys holiday for one week only for little more than enough pocket money to cover the week's board and lodgings.

Well here I am over eight decades later, and maybe another while yet, for at least half of which dainty little Alice Murphy remained a tender Godmother all her life, most frequently in the early days with a generous silver sixpence for a seat in the Cosy Corner Picture House, a bag of ten wrapped toffees and an ice cream wafer, a "slider", on the way home. The 'Thirties were an unique period of fiscal deflation, a farthing would buy four wrapped sweets, since when I would rarely ever again enjoy such orgiastic indulgence, except perhaps when it was free, and we reaped the harvest of progging the bankrupt orchards of Armagh until the world war claimed them for food.

CHAPTER TWO

The Boy Steps Out or to Macroom and Back

I, Christened and Confirmed as Patrick Joseph McGarvey, herein after just plain Paddy McGarvey, and for four years, the ward of a cardinal, can only be one of the most remarkable Irishmen of the twentieth century. I expect a statue marking my exploits and fame will be erected early in this 21st century, but not just yet. I would like it to be placed in front of Armagh Gaol, where my mother was born, facing The Mall and pointing to the long meadow grass left uncut at the eastern end where she used to play with her brothers and sister, and where I hope my ashes will be scattered. As her family increased and grew, they over-crowded the prison house which was James's tenancy as Front Hall Officer. It is still there on the right, just inside the prison railings. They moved across the square to a handsome three storey house in Mall View Terrace. A prison warder residing at a fairly posh ribbon of The Mall with a wife and seven children, and betimes the lodger who would become my father, has a simple explanation, as I have partly explained. The wife had the money. My granny, inherited a farm near Tullamore, Kings County, from her Presbyterian parents who had (obviously) forgiven her for marrying a penniless Fenian soldier in the Royal Dublin Fusiliers. James was just back from anchoring Sudan to a unique Anglo-French mandate of Egypt via the battle of Tel el Kebir in 1882. Lasting only thirty minutes between a heavily armoured Scottish division to which the Dubs were attached, and a long vulnerable line of Egyptian volunteer rebels, it had a much wider result in easing the more rapid expansion of Britain's Empire. Perfidious Albion had tried to stop the

French building the Suez Canal, but now controlled it. Even today some Brits will blandly tell you that the Empire was mostly an accident which fortunately fell into their civilised hands.

Young James, still in his early twenties, got a job in Her Majesty's prisons thanks to his six years service on the Reserve, enabling him to marry, with whatever level of charm and chutzpah was needed, a comfortably off farmer's daughter. They had work stations at the town now called Portlaoise, followed by Dundalk, and finally for them, Armagh's regally sited pre-Napoleonic prison facing down the most beautiful urban centre in provincial Ireland. It now looks like a slightly damaged dowager duchess rudely elbowed by a crude vehicular entrance to a middle class British supermarket and car park. The Mall's paths and greens nevertheless still provide Armagh with an urban haven no other provincial towns in these islands can match. From the 18th century into the 19th, three wealthy and powerful Protestant primates, Robinson and the tandem Beresford cousins, lifted the mud-wall and thatch cattle town to a regional slate and marble capital city of civic and scientific grandeur—an Observatory and a recording Library included.

That aura has faded, thanks but no thanks this time to deep-laid Protestant insecurity, most memorably the decision to keep a second Ulster university well within Unionist parish bounds at Coleraine, way up on the north Antrim coast.

When P.J. died, in March 1942, leaving three orphans by ages 18, 14 and 10 there was a housekeeper living across the street who daily attended to our needs, plebian affairs that need not be detailed here, except for the most important one.

As minors still too young to own our house, it was held in trust for us in a loose Irish sort of way by a member of the Northern Ireland senate, soon to be the Nationalist leader there, James G. "Gerry" Lennon, a near relative; our fathers were cousins, Gerry Lennon was a trial lawyer of immense reputation. One-eyed from a childhood accident, his courtroom voice faintly but distinctly echoed the accent of his German mother. Gerry was beloved in Armagh as a solicitor to more of the poor than the powerful. His appearances in defence presented special problems to police and Crown prosecutors; the Resident Magistrates (unlike in England, salaried and qualified) liked him in their courts; judges nodded to him over the heads of counsel. Two nights before he died he was seen driving round the blacked-out security-gated streets in his Austin Westminster at two in the morning. He was looking for a youth whose mother had just phoned him at that hour to tell him her "wee son" was missing. The reprobate was found at daylight, unharmed by anything worse than his last drink. Our family mentor was at all times a tribune of the poor.

Between the law and the Senate, where he took over the party's leadership from the Armagh auctioneer Thomas McLaughlin, my father's best man, he could not always be around for us on any day to day basis. That position was taken on by a most surprising volunteer (so most would concur). Joseph P. MacRory, Cardinal Archbishop of Armagh, Primate of All Ireland since 1928, appointed himself as our guardian. He was 81 at the time. There are no legal papers pertaining to this appointment; he just sort of appointed himself by himself. My first impression of him, just before the war and I was ten, was of a stern crag-faced prelate standing on the front-door steps of his cathedral. In walkabout navy soutane, trimmed with red piping, and his crimson skull cap, he was alone save for my father and myself; it must have been a no-school day for me or a Saturday, and my father had taken me to witness an event he must have thought would stay in my memory, as it has.

He was there in his other main role as press aide to his third Cardinal, unpaid at source, but lineage earning from some of the newspapers for which he wrote episcopal news. So we watched as a long black Austin Fourteen pulled in through the street gates and stopped. From our front door perch high above, a woman could be seen getting out of it and paying the driver, turning to commence the exacting ascent of the seven terraces of steps. It was obvious that this was something she wanted to do, rather than simply stay in the car for the easy drive encircling the cathedral. As she got nearer I beheld a tall lady of some years attired entirely in a dark grey woollen suit, the skirt down to just above her ankles, so no ordinary nun, though a bonnet with a grey veil to her shoulder indicated something akin to nuns, a nurse, perhaps—a bit of both actually. She gave a little courtesy to the Cardinal as he handed her a script from Rome, or maybe one of his own, authorising her to commence in Ireland, what she had previously launched in Port Harcourt, Africa, the Medical Missionaries of Mary. Grey Lady was their founder, Mother Mary Martin. She gave me a beatific smile and reached into her purse, also woollen, hanging at her hip, and handed me, to my vivid and visible disappointment, a religious medal. Unworthy of me I know, a witness to Ireland's history, I thought it might have been a half crown at least. After all, she had only paid the taxi to the gates and walked the rest. Many years later, reading their website, I was shamed to see she had nearly died in Africa. The climb to Armagh cathedral must have been just that little extra act of thanksgiving. I made my own, thirty years later, at the gates of the hospital she built in Drogheda. While the rest of Fleet Street was combing the Left Bank in Paris and the kibutzims of Israel looking for a jilted London prima ballerina who had vanished, I was interviewing Mother R, the hospital's official spokesperson, in their gatehouse in Drogheda. She was rubbishing my concrete tip, that the forlorn dancer was there, as an aspiring novice, or just seeking solace of the breach with her titled swain. Quite suddenly a small Tipperary coach rolled in past the gatehouse and disgorged six or seven white-clad novices, laughing in chatter as they made their way to the convent, down the drive. Despite their loose ankle-length habits, designed to cover everything feminine in the body, it was not too difficult to notice the one who's hips made a visible demonstration from left to right, while her feet were angled sharply outward in her graceful walk. I silently pointed out her retreating *forme* to crimson-faced Mother R, resolute nevertheless: "But Mr. McGarvey, you are about to destroy her life again."

But I didn't. I made an excuse and left, visiting a few friends before flying back to the street of shame. I abandoned around £500 in freelance earnings. Many times since I have guessed, well, hoped, she's praying for me, still, wherever she is.

More recently I also Googled my very own Cardinal, and stumbled into this. The same year he took over the young McGarveys, which was also the year he had rejected the pleas of Roosevelt and Churchill's ambassadors in Armagh to allow conscription in the North for British forces, for Catholics, and thus for all, this brief acerbic cameo by TIME magazine appeared a few months later on October 12 1942.

I can never forget what we in, Ireland owe to the Catholics of New York and other American cities. So said doughty, blue-eyed Joseph Cardinal MacRory, Roman Catholic Archbishop of Armagh and Primate of All Ireland, when he visited the U.S. in 1935. Last week the 81-year-old Cardinal addressed Americans in a different fashion. He found it "exceedingly hard to be patient," he complained, when he thought of "my own corner of my country overrun by British and U.S. soldiers against the will of the nation." By "my own corner" the Cardinal meant 66% Protestant Ulster, where he was born, lives.

Like many another Irish leader, Cardinal MacRory has leaned so far backward in his effort to be neutral that his head sometimes seems to be in the Third Reich. In 1938 he ordered public prayer "for Christians in Germany who are being subjected to a most dangerous persecution," but since the war's outbreak he has reserved his most vigorous denunciations for the Allies.

Cardinal MacRory is a graduate of Maynooth, famed Irish seminary which has sent priests all over the world. He taught there for 26 years before becoming a bishop in 1915. In 1928 he was appointed to St. Patrick's see, got his red hat in 1929. A sharp-tongued Irishman who never minces his words, the Cardinal has positive dislikes—among them, Protestantism ("the Protestant Church here and elsewhere is no part of the Church which Christ founded") and modern civilization (which "increases the opportunity for sin").

A holy terror, eh? Well for Protestants anyway. It was from an Armagh enriched by the influx of foreign troops from Britain, Canada, America and Belgium throughout the second world war, its population swollen from 9,000 to 15,000, that I Paddy, the ward of that same Cardinal, emigrated in January 1946 to far off County Cork in search of fame and fortune in journalism. The worst war in history had ended only months before. The world lay silent and weary, counting the dead by the million. I was enraptured.

My destination was Macroom, twenty five miles west of Cork city, population 2000, where I would commence a district news-gathering role for The Southern Star's home newsroom in far off Skibbereen, well, about forty miles say. The paper's new owner, Joseph O'Reagan, a former creamery owner, (in Britain, a dairy) met me at Cork rail terminus wheeling a bicycle. I thought he was somebody going somewhere, but he naturally recognised the downy cheeked stripling straining with his father's bulging Gladstone bag. We shook hands, and he said, "Here, you'll need this where you are going," handing me the bike. For a moment I had the horrors he wanted me to cycle the 25 miles to Macroom, me the cruelly deprived younger brother denied a ride on his big brother's. Five miles anywhere would finish me. My alarm was momentary; just outside the station in McCurtain Street a skinny undernourished little man in conductor's uniform marched up to us, saluting Mr. O'Reagan, and lifted the bicycle in one hand with surprising ease and shinnied up on the back-of-the-bus steps they all had in those days. With an awe inspiring wave he swung it up and over, still with only one hand, onto the roof. My proprietor handed me a list of names, beginning with my lodgings, and the important people in Macroom to whom I must make myself known.

A tingle of excitement raced down my neck as I boarded a bus with the destination Killarney, so famous in song and fable. It continued as the bus trundled through the centre of Ireland's third city; crossing Patrick Bridge with the visual drama of huge war-painted Atlantic cargo ships so close in on the Lee berths. The zig-zagging 'Parna'—the local argot for

Patrick Street' I would soon make the centre of my universe, at least one day a week working up my column, I Cover Cork City (By the famous columnist aged 18!)

The downside, the first gnawing doubts, sank to my stomach about an hour or so later with the opening views of my destination, rolling into the eastern outskirts of a town that must have resembled Armagh before the archbishops took over about 1790. The thatch on a long line of one-storey terraced cabins hung over the pavements in tatters. The street looked and felt as if it had been ploughed, the bus thumping and banging its sump on the street's unending saddle hump. I was reminded of a famous photo of the Great War, a Flanders village through which a hostile army had passed. Passengers lurching left and right and left again bumped their heads on the windows while gripping the seats in front for fear. I would learn the cause later—it made some of my opening stories—but at that stage I felt I had made a terrible mistake and could not wait for the bus to stop, jump off and arrange my journey home; Mr. O'Reagan's bike could end up in Killarney for all I cared. The spectacle of decay and neglect moderated to tidy, clean streets as we reached the centre, still clinging to the promise of its Victorian hey day of offices, pubs and shops. Just before reaching the busier square, the street still narrow, the bus pulled up at one of the shops for parcel deliveries. A few people got off, the Armagh traveller close behind them. I had made up my mind, no deal, no way, not here, not my kind of town. I stepped down heavily with my suitcase and turned to tell the conductor he could have my bike until the paper retrieved it. A roly-poly little woman stepped forward from the shop door beaming from a wide smile and a welcoming outstretched hand, to which I could only respond with my left hand.

She held on to it, obliging me to drop the suitcase from my right hand to the pavement, from which it seemed to leap into her left hand and she was leading me into the shop, my left hand now warmly and tightly in hers.

"Welcome to Macroom Mister McGarvey. You must be very tired now, such a young man even so, sure you're hardly a mister at all, only a boy and you after travelling all this way to us. Come in now and sit down and rest yourself and sure the kettle is on for a nice pot of tea and whatever you fancy with it."

(In retrospect I have long since felt that the immature teenager who had lost his mother at six was at that moment caught up in this warm-voiced lady's effusion of motherly care) Bewilderment, shock even, must have registered all the way up from my hanging jaw to my widened eyes. The rapid intuition that would drive my journalism to random bursts of success took over, and I twigged. It was a fit-up; the bus had stopped at the Main Street door of my digs as pre-arranged, the driver fixed by Mr. O'Reagan without question This pre-booked landlady would naturally recognise the youth who stepped off the bus at her door. *She even knew my name you blockhead!* The bus conductor, no doubt with a share of the "fix", was already dancing on the roof to extricate my bike, a bus-top ballerina indeed, the like of which we never see now. As the bike bounced hard on the pavement, making a crowd with my luggage, a micro-second of doubt intervened. Mrs. Bridget O'Sullivan, a shopkeeper across a marble counter crowned with a bacon slicer, serving butter and eggs as well, had just at that moment appointed herself mother to the son she never had with her two daughters. A man with a bristly moustache, her husband "Denny", wheeled my bike through the shop and house to the back yard and I was home. Then the bus driver dismounted, came round and shook my hand and wished me well. So did the conductor, refusing my clumsy attempt to slip him a sixpence. They had all heard about my job and were looking forward to reading all about Macroom in the Star.

After two years law clerking for gentle, kind Vincent Mulholland, who had headhunted me from school, and had taught me to write sentences beginning *that this indenture witnesseth,* fate had decreed I would never be a star at the Bar, but here instead, a star on the Star. The first, essential qualification for journalism is self-belief, an asset with which I was richly endowed, thanks only to a vivid imagination, no fees or entrance exams required. Looking around at the co-conspirators I did have a sense of being dragooned, but being warmly fussed over as well.

Before we went in, I noticed other shopkeepers standing smiling at their doors; the arrival of the bus had caused the commotion. What had happened might just as easily have occurred in Armagh or Antrim, yet there was something different here, in this isolated town of broken roofs and ruptured streets. It lay in the air like an embracing balm applied especially to strangers, and was there long before a ground-breaking Tourist Board needed to invent it for everywhere else. There are no other words for it than West Cork Hospitality, its unique quality now known the world over. And yet, as I was also soon to find, there had been a war here, recent enough to be in the memory of many I would meet.

Just over twenty five years before, the British army and its even more unwelcome police irregulars, the "Black and Tans" found themselves confronting their most ruthless enemy only months after the Great War, here. But that was then, and this was now, and the now was extraordinary. Elsewhere I tell the story of acquiring a motorbike and the struggle that followed to find a battery for it, in a place and time for whole towns to run out of petrol. Who would service it for me? I was told—I cloak the name—"Oh that'll be Bertie Smithers, he's your man for motorbikes."

By then a daily name-taking newsman among West Cork's distinctive clans of Twomeys, Twohigs, O'Sullivans, O'Learys and the like, I exclaimed: "Bertie Smithers! That's a strange name around here."

There was an eye-rolled grin, then a tilt of the head and a pause, the signal for the Cork mood of concession. Something was about to be admitted.

Ah well, you see, "he was a Tan right enough, but he married a grand girl and sure that was that."

A Black and Tan in West Cork marries a local cailin and gets away with it? I goggled in amazement. The response was Cork cool. "T'was just the way of it, so; she might have had about ten admirers, that girl, and when the one turned out to be the fella he was, not one of them would put harm her way"—not exactly what you read in histories. There was a pause, then: "It wasn't a killing thing at all, never."

I remember a pang of sadness. What a pity they did not afford such forgiving grace to the one of their own who founded modern Ireland? Because this also happened;. On a darkening fair day in that first February I have my notebook out to scribble prices and I'm tapped on the shoulder by a man in a long black Ulster overcoat leaning on a stout cattle stick. He orders: "Will you put down there that my mother was a first cousin of Michael Collins." Three times in ten months I had that.

Collins came to Armagh to fight for the parliamentary seat in 1918; sadly I suspect my father did not take to him, a veteran member missing from the group picture with the Nationalist-led council and Sinn Fein supporters. He did not win it. A time when you could register for more than one seat, he was returned in North Cork. He would never have been at ease representing a struggling mill town such as Armagh was.

The Mill Row boys in their patched and straggly hand-me-down trousers and torn jerseys were always first at Monday's Cosy Corner cinema—somehow. In Railway Street we would raise questioning looks to the ten or twenty of them as these most acerbic critics marched home again, a laughing band of slum brothers in flesh and spirit: "It's a bake Paddy, don't bother, a real bake" they chorused in "fake" poetry, They had probably chatted loudly throughout a Charles Boyer and Claudette Colbert dialogue . . . The Commissionaire, Jim Magee, in bright blue uniform of stripes and epaulettes more redolent of an admiral in the Peruvian navy, would have flashed his torch over them in vain: "Quiet there now, this is a melodrama".

We did go to that picture, Daddy, Jimmy and I. During the Boyer-Colbert encounter in a kitchen the morning after and Hollywood Frenchman was apologising for his poor behaviour the night before, my father awoke from slumber, rose to his feet, and berated Boyer as a bounder and malcontent. He received an ovation from the thrupennys all the way up to the one and thrupennys in the balcony.

John O'Connor's Mill Row scenarios were equally sparing, yet richly demonstrative, a strikingly handsome Post Office telegram teenager on a bike who could write. I badly wanted to be like him. Jimmy entered me in the Post Office entrance exam. I came first telegram boy in the UK, but meantime the Cardinal had put me down for the Hibernian Bank, in which he held honorary rank. To their directors this was an imprimatur. P. McGarvey, Civic Hibernus Sum. They sent me a booklet on how to behave and dress while working in such august surrounds. I rejected their diktat on dress and told Jimmy to tell the Cardinal I couldn't count. By then John O'Connor had written a prize-winning novel of life in Mill Row, a grim and funny factory avenue of unemployed people—Come Day Go Day.

My favourite memory of Come Day.

Son: "Mammy?"
Mother: "Whatey?"

The weariness of impoverished motherhood, and love, leap from just two words. John died young visiting Australia, choking during a meal he was sharing with friends. I remember the loss I felt, even wishing, selfish, if only I had his typewriter, I might be able to emulate him.

My first Cork friend was Gerry T, in his early twenties a mint-fresh member of the Garda Siochana. The District Court was run on much the same lines as it was then in the North, where as Vincent Mulholland's clerk, I had attended Armagh and Keady Petty Sessions in charge of documentation and witness statements—and watching the journalists. Both court systems used appointed stipendary magistrates. Gerry was frequently the courtroom officer, helping with passing round documents or witness exhibits. Outside we found mutual interest in each other patrolling the Fair Day, me in search of stories and prices.

The brick and slate town centre facing Macroom Castle around the square, shares crowded humanity on fair days with the livestock of the fields, cattle, fowls, and fodder in the shape of huge bundles of kale. My Armagh accent grates on Cork ears with momentary smiles of surprise, followed by impeccable manners across the gaps of misunderstanding. Gerry appoints himself as translator, an excuse to join the craic. Quite suddenly there is a commotion in the crowd, a horse coper is running a skittish young mare towards us at a canter. It is a wonderful thing to see, because he is matching her stride, step by step with his. One thing we were all supposed to know, even me, you must never interrupt the harmony of this exercise. One misstep and the coper could easily break the horse's rhythm, and worse, its breathing might slip to one lung at a time, revealing for all to hear "a whistler"—a sale disaster.

I knew all about that mind you (I told you I was exceptional) through seeing horse sales at Moy, five miles from Armagh, the very pretty village known to all and sundry as "The Moy" (Horse-Fair understood). Sure didn't I see some of Hitler's officers there buying Irish drays for the coming campaigns across Poland and Russia. I saw the other end of this story in the Cosy Corner Cinema, our great wee house of great epics, when a British newsreel commentator was showing struggling, over-laden horses at the siege of Leningrad (now restored as St. Petersburg) the commentator cried—"Neutral Ireland might not now be so neutral when they see Germans brutally flogging their pack horses across this frozen lake. The cinema erupted in noise and near riots before attendant Jim Magee could smooth them all down again.

Not all of these memories were fleeting though my shocked mind as I picked myself up from the skeins of wet mud and semi-skimmed manure, and brushing it off the new Burberry raincoat the dutiful big brother had bought me. In the big rush to get out of the way Guard Gerry cannoned into me. I went down like a bowling pin, him on top as he vainly tried to save me (he said). Left behind on the ground, as we both got upright—a dark, glistening revolver coated in British gunmetal-grey.

"My God" I exclaimed aloud enough for half the town to hear (Armagh accent with added brio con tremulo) "where did that come from?"

"Oh my God" Gerry replied sharply. "It's mine."

He flipped it very quickly into a tunic pocket. You couldn't be too careful. Only 23 years after the Civil War, Ireland still lingered with men who had stashed arms at home, wishing to emulate Michael Collins, or kill his state supporters, you could never tell. A few of the "boys", the ones aged about fifty, were grinning. Had we walked away without noticing, it would have been finders keepers, and Gerry on a charge back in the barracks. But the Garda Siochana was an unarmed force, so he had to have an explanation.

"Tis just the Ministry of Agriculture regulations on the Fair Day" and in response to my unspoken, he added "Like in case a cow would go mad and you had to shoot it."

I made the observation that the Royal Ulster Constabulary up north wear forty-fives in holsters, fair day or no fair day, even on traffic point duty. It was a political thing, a wee message to keep the more impulsive Catholics in their place.

"Forty-fives!" said Gerry. "This is only a thirty-eight", extracting it from his pocket again for all to see. He broke the magazine from the stock. Gerry knew how to handle it, like. All the chambers were empty. "It's empty" I jeered, laughing as well. "You have no bullets, have you?"

Young Guard T looked at me the way my brother does, as if I was the original Irish omadaun—a gormless idiot in the English that is—clearly just in from the bogs.

"For God's sake Pat, what would I want with bullets, sure who ever heard of a cow going mad?"

I was in Cork from that moment on, and have understood and loved them ever since. (nearly a whole year I spent there, and they never called me Paddy).

I had other lessons in life from Macroom Garda. Best remembered since, recounted many times in bed, usually to someone else in it, was my encounter with a profound sergeant at the scene of a drowning. Barely a mile east of the town, the Killarney-Cork road breasts a rocky escarpment on a bridge that has to span the confluence of three rivers. The short foaming Laney splashes noisily into the more serene Sullane only yards before it sweeps grandly into the sluggish Lee, which barely thirty miles on, splits in two across Munster's capital, reforming into Ireland's deepest natural harbour. It is deep enough to shelter an Atlantic Cunarder

It was then a magical transformation of the three rivers, now interrupted, sadly some say, by the wondrously beautiful former waterlands of Inchigeela, further along the Lee valley, arrested by a dam. A flood plain adjoining the bridge often accommodated a gypsy camp. In a flash flood a woman had drowned and when she was found more than a week later a young Guard had fainted when trying to pull the partly decomposed body from the entangled broken branches of a fallen tree. The sergeant was explaining to me that the Laney was the principal culprit, cascading rapidly down the valley with great force after heavy rain in the Derrynasaggart Mountains. When the torrent blocked the bridge with broken tree limbs and mud, the water backed over the camp site.

He pointed away to the mountains in the north-west. Given extra authority by his huge caped raincoat, he indicated two perfectly matched peaks, each with smaller matching mounds on top, called The Paps.

"When heavy rain hits those two it's lookout for everybody along the Laney, game trout you can see in it one day, the next day it's a muddy killer.

"Sergeant" (Awkward Ulster argot again) "whey are they called the Paps?"

He gave me the dart of his eye, like I was having him on or what, but I wasn't, a decent Irish Catholic boy, educated, cautiously, by the Christian Brothers. About women themselves we knew nothing.

In measured tones, he delivered himself in words engraved in the memory of my youth and the years of parenthood. "Well now, you are a young man yet (*18 and one sixth actually*) but I have no doubt in the way of things, a presentable young man such as you are, will one day meet a fine girl and you'll be married in good time and sure enough, you will find out for yourself why those two mountains are called The Paps."

Policemen are not all like that. I was coming down the long straight hill from the west into Ballingeary one darkening September evening when a wild donkey leapt across my path, clouting the rump of my swerving BSA 500. Not for the first time was my motorcycling life saved by a spongy Irish ditch which then accepted a deep sculptural impression from my flying body, leaving all bones intact. When I regained the road, and struggled to lift the heaviest bike then around, I discovered I had no lights.

Cautiously. I walked the bike to the edge of the village where a single lamp might illuminate what was wrong. What was wrong with the lamp was the thin cadaverous Guard standing under it, notebook in hand, in which he proceeded to book me for no lights. The boyo had seen me coming, his day in court at last.

"Look here" I protested in my assumed magisterial tones, "why are you not doing something about stray donkeys running along the roads. I was nearly killed, so I was"

"I'll tell you why, young master from the North now, that donkey had the right of way long before you came here with your grand northern manner of speaking to the likes of us."

Gerry T he wasn't, nor the Sergeant who knew what I would find on my wedding night (actually a bit before that I must confess) but the leaves were in the wind. I was to leave Cork soon afterwards, and never did pay that fine.

So this, not my last story from the town where I made lifelong friendships, is how I got my motorbike, and how I got it running, as I am sure you are asking. I bought the spanking new bike in British khaki drab colours for £25 at an army-surplus sale in Ballincollig Barracks on the outskirts of the city. It was mint-fresh and unused by the Irish army getting it from the beleaguered British (Dunkirk still to come) just in case the Germans came by that way as so many strategists on both islands thought they might. A likely Irish Army view "Our lads would need some stuff to hold them back for a while until the British regrouped to drive the Germans back into the sea."

Strategists in Ireland, not all of them muddle-heads from the straggles of the IRA, thought the opposite would happen, and that Hitler would immediately hand ALL of Ireland back to us poor downtrodden Irish, the fine dacent man that he was. That view persisted right through to D-Day.

My 500cc BSA cost only £25, because it came without a battery, and a month's search of every dealer and garage within twenty miles was fruitless. Ah but, says you, where did this fella on £2 a week get £25. Well a little bit of savings, some gifts from home, and my deep undeclared love for a bank manager's beautiful daughter, a strawberry blonde called "C," which won me a £5 bank loan when she brought me upstairs to meet Daddy. Once more, you see, I impressed the parents. The rest was on hire purchase. I had a dead motorbike until the Man for Heinz 57 came into my lodgings.

Mrs O'Sullivan seats her two important guests at the same table. This was a special event for me as I was frequently late for meals in the nature of my job. When I was very late I always knew the greeting I would get from her: "I'll get a stick and bate you." But it was also her reproof that I had not eaten. She had no stick, she was telling me, therefore, the warmth in her voice, the smile that followed, she would not be able to whop me today.

Across the table your man explains he's on a field trip to persuade Munster farmers to grow peas and carrots to supply a canning factory they were going to open in Limerick. Heinz, the world's biggest food canner, had not thought of telling the local newspapers. There was no such thing as planned public relations in provincial Ireland of that time, and so Mr. Heinz at our lunch table was charmed when the ace reporter offered to remedy that with a story. About a week after my exciting tale was published, the Heinz rover was back in the digs offering me a fiver as a reward.

No, no, no, I incorruptly rejected the big white Bank of England note of the kind which would one day fracture my career with the Dublin Evening Mail, and asked instead. "Any chance, back in England, you could find me a Lucas Six Volt."?

A week later a stout wooden Heinz butter box was opened with great effort and some ceremony at the O'Sullivan doorstep, and there it was, a gleaming black, red-rimmed jewel of a darling battery. Half the shopkeepers in Macroom were gathered round as I fitted it to my bike, gave one kick and it roared into life. The local garage where I had it serviced actually told me it needed running in. No money was involved, so this was a bribe too—but only a mere thirty bob. Saved, a fifteen mile ride on my bicycle to Coachford and Crookstown, the same on another day to Ballyvourney and checking the distinguished guests in the two rival hotels run by two rival brothers in beautiful, haunting Gougane Bearra. I was the made man, king of the road, with a day to spare in Cork city for column material, I Cover Cork City, but wait until you hear this. All this was in March or April. The following October the paper's owner Mr. O'Reagan sacked me for my petrol bills, too expensive, he had no other excuse, and I was more puzzled than shocked. My arrival had spurred sales in the town's main paper shop, from seven copies to seventy and rising, so the owner told me. How many journalists can boast of achieving a 400% rise in circulation for their papers? The answer—none. (I did forewarn you I am an exceptional Irishman). The reality, as explained in The Star's centenary magazine of 1989, Joseph O'Reagan was facing a courtroom tussle with a rival shareholder for outright ownership, which he achieved the following year. I have no doubt since then I was dispensed with to clear the decks for that struggle, not the only time I got the boot for reasons beyond my own achievements in print. I bore no malice towards my first newspaper. Nearly 50 years later his son Liam, one of Ireland's best editor-leader writers, gave me £100, by way of a travel aide, he said. It was invested in the beginnings of Irish Parliament Trust.

Cork and Bristol, triple-centre cities divided twice by the rivers Lee and Avon, are my favourite urban areas in these islands; overseas, Florence holds that place in my heart on both sides of the tidal Arno, but Macroom is a place apart for its people. Mrs. O'Sullivan cut seven shillings and sixpence a week from my full-board lodging of 37s 6d a week when she rumbled I had only half a crown left in my pocket. Maybe she was hoping, I used to jest at the time, I would take Teresa to the pictures more often than twice, neither of us liking the seats with no backs. They made it so easy to fall into the laps of the people behind, the start they said, of many a romance in west Cork. If her mother actually thought that, it was not to be, as buddies we remained, Teresa articulately more intelligent than me, she the sarcastic Cervantes to this Don Quixote on his motor bike living up to the prevailing image of his schooldays, Big Head. As for the town itself, its roads so damaged by endless wartime convoys of turf lorries from Kerry to keep Cork city alive, it could only improve and it did

Thirty years on, in the 'Seventies and living back in Ireland on a peace mission, my second of three returns to my disturbed island, Macroom was Ship-Shape and Bristol Fashion with fresh paint, attractive shops, smoothed roadways, an American satellite factory, maybe two, while away in the north, my birthplace, the ecclesiastic capital of Ireland, was a shambles of bombed ruins, abandoned streets, economic despair, the steel-shuttered shops an obvious deterrent to any kind of social life after six.

The week after I was sacked I got a job on The Cork Examiner. For a start, it was a bit like that Lloyd George thing. The News Editor, Ned Russell, knew my father. He never actually met him; he just knew him as the reliable author of despatches on the country's religious affairs, hot news from Armagh, Catholic almost exclusively, until tiny, big-hearted Dr. Otto Simms came to Armagh's Protestant chair and took my brother Jimmy into his confidence for news briefings. Mr. Russell was amazed to find a callow looking 18-year-old as the author of a weekly column that often front-guessed the bigger city paper. He hired me as a news reporter and I went home to Macroom and a hullabaloo of a cellar party a few doors from the digs the following night, thrown for me by one of my column subjects, the immortal Joe Lynch and his stage "Jeff", Charlie McCarthy, the first to become a star of radio drama and TV, Charlie after an acting career to become a trade union leader. The following morning, recovering from my first hangover, I received a message from Mr. Russell asking me to call again as soon as possible. So I did. It was now his turn to sack me. The owners had failed to tell their own news editor they were about to land him with a favoured son, who had decided he wanted to be a journalist rather than take on the business end, and that was that. Mr. Russell extended the apologies of the Crosbie family with a twenty pound note, a very rare item of currency at the time, a generous ten times my weekly wage. The twenty quid absorbed the hurt feelings of saying goodbye to Macroom friends for good this time, as I naturally thought. A much greater shock was awaiting me in Armagh. Ireland's holy capital was in the grip of a frightening epidemic—typhoid. My brother Jimmy and my sister Nuala were taken to the emergency fever hospital before I got there. It killed eleven people across creeds and class, but young, strong, and caught in time, my only home kin survived, with the curiosity of different hair colour and styles. I was seemingly immune, but only because I had not been at home when the milk delivered daily from farm carts had been contaminated on one or two days. Milkmen crossing the domestic sales routes at the town centre had need to share milk supplies if a particular service had met extra calls. Here I must introduce another Jimmy—Jimmy the Baa, whose strange behaviour lightened my dark days back from Macroom.

Sergeant James Nethercott was stationed in the Russell Street barracks of the Royal Ulster Constabulary from where he conducted a reign of putative terror on all the children of Armagh and quite a few of their elders as well. Though rarely seen out of uniform, he was a brilliant detective with an intuitive grasp of criminology at all the levels which confronted him. None were spared his overhanging presence, which for misbehaving children and older offenders, was considerable for one other reason. He was the tallest man in the RUC. None under five-foot nine at that time, he could tower over his comrades at somewhere near seven foot None dare ask exact. Not only that, the Sergeant exercised his authority in spite of a serious handicap for a policeman. His voice was pitched even higher than those of his youngest targets. Hence the nickname no one would dare voice in his presence, a universal figure of fun larded with a certain reserve. He was easy to imitate, but only when you were absolutely certain he wasn't around.

But here comes the rub, his principle allies in keeping crime in Armagh to an absolute minimum were the mothers of Armagh, hoping of course he would never darken their doorstep. An obstreperous tearaway, a bully, a penny-nicking thief, a school mitcher (getting close to myself here) would be threatened with his presence, an "or else" to behave by their own mothers (in my case Granny Mullaly).

"I'll get Jimmy the Baa to you."

They had more force when I returned; Cork mothers, by the way, had their own bogeyman for bold children, the stern and autocratic bishop, Dr. Daniel Cohanlon. His name forms a line in Michael Collins day diary as someone to be seen—he had just excommunicated the state-founding IRA leaders. A Cork mother warns her stroppy child: "I'll get Danny Boy to you."

As patients in the fever hospital recovered and were returned to eating cautious amounts of solid food, what they needed most, in the way of soft fruits and other delectable comestibles, not usually available, suddenly did. After a short interval, special consignments of contraband edibles arrived by devious deliveries; remember, this was barely eighteen months after the world war and rationing of many foods and goods would persist until the early 'Fifties. It was the reporter acting as a go-between to his brother and sister who discovered that the master-mind, the Mr. Big delivering the booty, yes you're ahead of me, was Jimmy the Baa. No questions were asked. What! Question "our" Jimmy. Not on your Nellie was the way it was put at the time. But the end of this story is mystery, and somehow beyond the sadness of the eleven dead in the outbreak. This deeply Christian policeman took his own life, we heard years later. I haven't the slightest doubt as to where Sergeant James Nethercott is now, and I hope to see him again.

POSTSCRIPT 1951   The Slough Observer.

Leslie Tunks, the news editor, called me to his desk and asked me to write an obituary on a ninety year-old doctor who had just died. He lived most of his life in Colnbrook, a village wedged between Heathrow Airport and the town, its weekly news items part of my regular work. "He was famous" explained the paper's most formative future editor, "for breeding hackney ponies and unfortunately, just before you joined us, a bad fire at his stables killed 24 of them."

A tall, elegant lady of middle years in a neat boxy Chanel suit and soft cashmere sweater supporting a short string of pearls, let me in to join two other reporters. She was the doctor's daughter, introducing herself as Mrs. James Crosbie. "My husband is an Irish senator" she explained, a response I suppose to my name and accent "and everybody calls me that."

She was pouring tea for us, me still silently digesting that astonishing news, and deciding to keep it to myself, but she was on to me when the thought struck her to ask for my name again. "And did you once get a job on our paper in Cork only to be sacked a day or two later?" My jaw was too near the floor for adequate speech and I could only nod as she went on anyway. "For years now I have worried and worried and worried about you. Only weeks after you were hired and dismissed, that young man who was very close to me fell in love with a girl who had been married before, and left the paper to join her in Nicaragua."

Very quietly I told Mrs. Crosbie that I would have had to leave the Cork Examiner a few weeks after joining, anyway, because my only family left, my brother and sister, were taken very seriously ill in the Armagh typhoid epidemic. When I told her they had made a complete recovery, she was doubly relieved. I felt unable to ask if the runaways were still happy. A few days after this astounding news that I was meant to hear,

I saw a girl cycling very slowly along a deserted Slough High Street. Her chocolate A-line skirt was draped back over the rear wheel. An olive blouse was buttoned to the neck supported by a tiny tartan bolero with tog straps that allowed her figure to flourish. Behind, or because of, a hooked nose, she was remarkably pretty. She was married. Her husband, George Lukic, a former Yugoslav soldier and a war prisoner of the Germans, linked to the exiled King Peter of Yugoslavia in London, had gone off to America with the king's Chetniks on a block visa, a sudden do or never decision his wife could not accept, remaining in England with their infant daughter, Averill. I would soon be in the same boat as the young Corkman who took my job. I hoped he was as happy as I eventually became, in spite of a 16-year diktat by Rome that the Serbian Orthodox Church, by which rite they were married, while in schism with Rome, 'is not in heresy'. Ergo, the marriage was rock solid valid by Rome. Civic Romanus Sum, I confessed in religious terms to my brother and sister in Armagh, flying back again to marry the girl at Kingsclere Register Office, Hampshire; if it's still there, you'll find it just down the road from "Downton Abbey". Posh, eh?

The name of her first husband struck me as odd from the start, remembering the cheerful little GI Pfc stationed with the US Second Division in Armagh before D-Day, who came visiting our house to see our young housekeeper, Kitty Hagan, and take her out on dates. He survived the war, writing letters to Kitty, and me as well, but he did not return to us, going home to Springfield, Illinois. His name? George Lukic!

Averill's father, who had been labouring in the foundations of London's new airport at Heathrow, found his true measure at Pittsburgh University, where he obtained a PhD in Slav Languages and Literature, remaining there as a fellow and don tuturing in Serbo-Croat languages, literature and culture, the university informs me. He retired in the early 80s.

In 1970, December 8, the Feast of the Immaculate Conception, Pam and I were conditionally married again in a crypt chapel of Westminster Cathedral, with all but two of our seven children around us, Averill at work, Conal at school in Ireland. Close friends, Fred and Maureen Hamilton, were best man and matron-of-honour for us. We were married downstairs, because I objected to upstairs, feeling the round dozen of us would have been lost in that towering canyon of Catholicism.

CHAPTER THREE

Big City Newsman. 1947

The Dublin of my holiday childhood and working youth had three urban icons that most distinguished the city from all others, Nelson's Pillar with its public staircase to the top; at its base began the Dalkey Tram "coming together like cheese and ham", while from the centre to the suburbs you could not walk far without meeting a baker's cart trundling behind a heavy Irish dray, to whom the skipping children in virtually every street, chanted

> Johnston, Mooney and O'Brien
> Bought a horse for one and nine
> When the horse began to kick
> Johnston Mooney bought a stick

One decade later I would carry my 18-month-old son Conal to the top of the Pillar, Averill and Shane just ahead of me, while Mama relaxed in the car parked at the base. Well, that was 1957. The Pillar was blown down by white French Algerian imperialists hired by Irish malcontents affronted by the symbol of British imperialism in the fair city, a sub-nascent IRA devoid of arms or ordinance paying the French equivalent of Ulster Loyalists to do the job for them. The Dalkey Tram and its sisters were banished to make room for the motor car, a mistake Dublin and some British cities are only recently rectifying. The beloved Bakers Three, their delicious dough, and their well-behaved horses, shrank under the weight of the spawning supermarkets.

Long before these sad events reduced Dublin to drab urban anonymity, I was pre-cool to all of them, by age 19 a fellow-about-town with a glamorous occupation, a confident sophisticate of the metropolis, a star reporter on the Dublin Evening Mail, well by age at least, and that was merely the day job. As a great carillon of city bells rang out across the holiest Christian city north of Rome, to remind the Faithful to say the Angelus, as does the State Radio and TV to this day, I was climbing the worn, seedy stairs to the newsroom of Eamon DeValera's morning paper, The Irish Press. Ahead of me lay another four hours of "Night Town", this after a full day's work begun at 9:30 a.m. around the bullet-riddled reporters's table in the Mail newsroom, before departing for a day of covering civil law cases in the Four Courts by hourly hand-written accounts of a case for Mail messengers.

So, barely two years out of an Armagh solicitor's office where gentle, patient Vincent Mulholland taught me land equity and how to write sale covenants beginning *That This Indenture Witnesseth,* the capital city of some of the Irish lay four square at my feet, and me rarely richer ever since. Casually employed on both papers, I was earning in the law terms a guinea and a half per day at the Mail; that is £1.11s 6d, then half of that for the four hours at the Press, 15s 9d, totalling £12 2s 3d for a five-day week. When the Press began offering Sunday all—day shifts my weekly income rose frequently to £15—a cool sixty bucks in Stateside money. Part-board and lodgings in 1947 for £2 a week in Percy Place, on the fringe of crumbling Ballsbridge, included a ploughman's breakfast, a cooked high tea and laundry. Croesus rich I was—in the law terms. So I had time and the money for the town; the work was part of the fun anyway. These were days when you announced you were a news reporter and the response from the plain people of Ireland, Britain and America no different: "Oh, you must lead a wonderful life."

My Edwardian father's son, I dressed accordingly, but less Paddy McGarvey, to permit a touch of Mike the Pencil Sharpener. I still had my snap-brim brown trilby, made in shaggy Galway calfskin, bought in Cork, pulled low and raked like Robert Mitchum's in The Big Sleep, a military Burberry with straps and buckles like Humphrey Bogart's, the first to play Phillip Marlowe. It was suitably stained with nicotine and Bewley's coffee, worn collar up against the riveting, river-borne east wind at O'Connell Bridge. There I would pause to inspect the flocks of office and shop-girl cyclists stop and drop one leg, the other high on a pedal. The two traffic cops had a great time of it. I let the aromatic fumes of my exotic Turkish fags drift across the girls—the Sultan's incense to entice their questioning glances. Twenty Players Navy Cut or Wills Gold Flake of mass popularity cost 1s 9d; my Balkan Sobranje 4s 9p. As I said, I was a man's man on the town. Already I was shaving three times a week. Years after my cultivated Bogart look, my trade union, the NUJ, ran a series of recruitment posters in which the ace reporter in the chaotic newsroom was Bogey himself. I grinned in restrained mirth at this pointer to my recurring failure in journalism—being first, too fast on the draw, and far too soon.

The Evening Mail's entrance was in Parliament Street, but once upstairs the extended newsroom curled around the corner into Christchurch Street, its huge windows overlooked by the City Hall, overshadowed in turn from behind by the rear shoulders of Dublin Castle. It was on the Mail's rickety wooden staircase I received my confirmation in journalism. A web axle in the cramped machine room had to protrude through the wall of the staircase. You not only heard the press, you also had to duck left going up the stairs; today's health and safety mandarins would have had a blue fit. The combination of printing noise, the tremors of the building and the heavy smell of hot ink turned me on every time with racing blood and tingling neck. The printing shed of the world's largest Sunday paper, the News of the World, was a huge sub-basement at the bottom of Bouverie Street, opposite the News Chronicle building, my second London daily; on Friday evenings, when the London end of the seven-million print run had to start, I often got a "fix" hunkering down on the pavement to gaze in at five or six webs, all tended by machine minders waving their oil cans at the metal junctions.

The bullet holes in the Mail reporters's table were the harvest of crossfire between opponents in the 'Tan war, or the Civil War that succeeded it, neither version of which could be authenticated from any official source. The story presumed the shooting was exchanged between high windows in the Castle and a hotel further down Parliament Street. It was a talking point that added some historic respectability; it sort of brought the Protestant-owned paper into the authentic Catholic mainstream; they'd had a gun battle, they were one of us. The Mail was famed for its theatre critic, Bram Stoker, who from his house in Clontarf would invent Count Dracula. The Mail had its own special impact on the city. A comic strip featured a top-hat and evening-cloak detective who had magic powers of deduction—Mandrake. Anytime, anywhere, I mentioned to expatriate Dubliners I was on the Mail, they would often exclaim; "Ah, you weren't Mandrake, were ya?"

The paper closed down in 1962 after a failed commercial adoption by the Irish Times, itself nearly dead at the time.

My duties began at the front door for the walk down Parliament Street to Carlisle Bridge, then over the river and a few yards left to the Four Courts, a five-minute morning saunter. Leo Walsh, the only News Editor in my life I found to have been a daily communicant, made me guardian angel to an alcoholic colleague, respected and valued at work, once brought safely past the pubs that lay between.

"Michael" spoke in a soft Western accent, and was gentlemanly with it. He was dapper in appearance save that his jacket and waistcoat had a permanent patina of spilled ale and nicotine, to be fair, not an uncommon mode of Dublin male dress at the time. After a few runs with no trouble from him, I ventured to the News Desk that he could be safely sent off on his own. Most of the barmen in Parliament Street were still sweeping out through doors jammed open with bottle crates, while mounds of unsocial debris lay across the linoleum floors. An odour-mix of stale porter and itchy tobacco fumes struggled to survive the combined onslaught of Jeyes Fluid and Mansion Polish, all floating out across the narrow street like a cloud of old sins. It was a great relief to reach the bridge and breathe the natural pong from tide-out Anna Plurabella Liffibus (Was that from Gogarty or Joyce?). Scene and smell together would daunt the hardiest toper from even trying to step in past those crates, and besides, I had other things I wanted to do, says I, getting uppity. Mr. Walsh glared at me and slapped his roll-top desk with both hands. His was just like the one in the newsroom comedy, The Front Page "Now you listen to me Mr. McGarvey, if you take your eye off that fellow for an instant he'll have the barman's brush."

Leo Walsh gave ME the brush—twice. I survived the first to stay aboard, but not the second, foolish but innocent. Twenty years later in Dublin's rival Georgian city of Bath, a Banbridge foreman on the new university building shouted at me: "Let me see your hands you stupid bugger" On the roof of the fifth floor he had signalled me to help him lift a twenty-foot insulation plank made of cement and sawdust, with alloy-trimmed edges. Even just looking at it, I knew I could not do as he asked. He was the stupid one, standing at the other end of it within a foot of the edge and an eighty-foot drop to his death, if at the other end, I stumbled forward from the great weight. Inspecting the outstretched hands that should have been playing a Stradivarius at La Scala for Princess Grace Kelly, or sealing Princess Diana's broken heart valves in St. Bart's as an anxious nation waited, he yelled: "You're a bloody ringer you are. Who are you? Who sent you here?"

I was the Sunday Telegraph's ringer on the building sites, but I couldn't tell him that, and he handed me a sweeping brush that just happened to be lying there: "That's all you're good for, and collect your cards on Friday." I must be the only journalist of so many sacked in those years of News Desk power, long since relegated to the backroom bean counters, who also got the real, the genuine, original "brush off"

I digress a little more here to reveal a great trade secret of the Irish building gangs. My first early morning duty on the site was to start the mixer, left uncovered all night, the engine parts icy cold and drenched in dew; no way would it start under its maker's normal instructions. The laughing lads clocking-on past me uttered the same basic advice in a chorus of accents from Donegal to Waterford: "Piss on it Mate""

Banbridge foreman was looking daggers at me. I had to do something. A careful look round to make sure of some privacy, a fumble at my fly, I stood on tiptoe and aimed a spurt of *McGarvey 69* at the carburettor's bell-mouth. The condensation vanished under the caress of my first-day vintage; I swung the handle just the once, to hear the mixer grunt just the once, then two or three anxious seconds later, twice, and she was away. It was heard all over the site to sardonic cheers from the combined ranks of McAlpine Fusiliers, Wimpey's Wonderworkers, Laing's Legionaries. My heart warmed to them, the bastards. When Churchill was ranting at the Irish Peace Treaty negotiations about Britain's empire role, Collins interrupted him: "We too are a nation of empire builders." Some thought he was referring to the missioners, those brave holy people who in those days knew they would never come home again. I like to think he also meant the magnificent 'Micks'

Just yards from my Dublin lodgings,—"digs" in shabby, genteel Percy Place, stands a pretty little bridge over the Grand Canal, across which I turn right towards the junction of Lower Mount Street to begin my two mile walk to the Mail. Opposite to my citywards turn, was a large service garage with a low front wall which gave the crossroads area its name, Huet's Corner. The garage has long since vanished under an office unit. The building on my side was an older block of expensive apartments, altogether a busy place with tram stops in both directions. The noise of their grinding brakes, the wheel rumble when they start, and their zinging bells has to be imagined now. You just knew you were in a great metropolis, and this was its music. A few extra short bangs one sunny morn were nothing out of the ordinary That must have been my only excuse, apart from the air of dauntless self-importance in which I constantly embalmed myself, the ace reporter on the Mail, *never glad confident morning again,* well not in Dublin, going head up around this corner and not noticing. A gang of men in the flats were shooting at policemen lying behind Huet's two-foot garage wall, shooting back—allowing only time for a passing tram, and this passing ham.

I sauntered between them, my head high like Yeats just along this same route when he went round to consult AE a few doors away in Merrion Square, and passed poor old Russell coming to see him, head bent low. Their housekeepers told them each was at the other's. My housekeeper was raging.

A mile further on I turned in to Dame Street. It was nearly nine now and the city was stirring. A single small Ford Ten came whizzing along, braked hard, and U-turned across to my kerb. My Chief Reporter, James Doran O'Reilly was shouting: "How did you get through? Did you see the gun battle?" He made a go-away arm gesture of disgust to my stumbling mask of ignorance above my wide-open mouth, and sped away. About noon I was recalled from the Four Courts and walked back across the river and up the gentle slope of Parliament Street, up the Mail's throbbing staircase, for sure I was mounting the steps of the guillitine, Citizen McGarvey, fini. The rival Evening Herald was already in the streets, crying havoc. and selling papers faster than the boys running back for more. Told that my future would be discussed later, I had eight pennies in my pocket and used two of them to telephone Ma K to see if I could have lunch on tick until Friday. Was this the stricken orphan missing his Mother who sought his kind landlady's comfort in food, a share of good hot meat stew followed by baked apple and custard.?

Well maybe. This time as I strode out once more from Percy Place, there were two very tall Gardai on the bridge. I had walked past them with a smile and a nod when some instinct, some spark of desire for a restoration of self-respect on a shameful day, or just plain showing off again, I turned back to them: "Well gentlemen, I'm from the Evening Mail, though I'm usually in the Law Courts—so how's the gun battle going.? "There came a duet chorus in reply: (they must have mistook me for a lawyer) "Terrible, terrible so it is. We've just shot our own chief, shot him dead so we have. 'Tis terrible altogether, God save us." I gave them a barely audible giggle, waiting for the laugh, taking the piss out of this pompous fellow from the courts. The silence that followed was far too serious for a joke. The gun exchange had somehow moved down the canal, seaward and into a ship-repair works behind a high brick wall.

One of the Gardai put his two hands on the parapet: "Our lads were on this wall". With his left hand he then gestured along that bank of the canal "and the Superintendent went along to see if we could be got closer to the gang. Unfortunately the poor man found a latch gate in the wall, and when he opened it and stepped through for a look, one of our lads on this wall here, took aim and shot him."

I ran for a tram to get to the office, caught myself on, and tore back to beg use of my tolerant landlady's private phone I knew she had in the family front room. Walsh was so shocked he reproved me for my behaviour; he thought I was having him on. I gave him the Superintendent's name. When the Mail hit the streets with the headline killing of a senior police officer by one of his own men it shocked the City—and the Herald newsroom. I got a bonus—my job eased back. I remember schoolmasterly Walsh saying: "It seems Mr. McGarvey, you are different from the rest of us; you have two guardian angels." I would remember that the second time he fired me. That one was final, but even then, a lone guardian angel turned up, him, speechless.

A permanently briefless barrister of some aristocratic mien, and private means, used to prance around the Four Court lobbies with wads of old files under his arm. He never seemed to have any work. One day he confronted me and other journalists demanding we keep his name out of a drunk-driving case involving him, which had come in for appeal. He was terrified the Bar would silence his non-existent career. I laughed; I was not involved anyway. All my copy had gone, and his was not one of my cases. He had no worries I told him as I headed back to the office. He followed me as far as Carlisle Bridge, persisting, pleading, then he suddenly stuffed a skinny white pencil, as I thought, into my breast pocket and fled back to the courts. It unrolled in my hand into a huge Bank of England parchment fiver. I can see him still, the Westminster overcoat with the brown velvet collar, clutching his wig. Silly bugger, I thought; I'm not helping him. I can't help him. He's gone off, so I might as well keep it anyway As I entered the newsroom Leo Walsh was putting down the phone and barking at me: "*Have you just now taken a five pound bribe from a barrister?*" Coming up the vibrating stairs I had been fretting whether to tell him or not. Blustering, explaining, too late now, I was finished. Bloody briefless barrister, displaying the sheer stupidity that kept him in that state, had phoned to confirm his investment, with any which way a result the opposite of his intention. What follows is an unforgettable night followed by an unbelievable morning. What else had happened in the newsroom is a total blank. I did not seek my landlady's sympathy this time. I did not go anywhere with any purpose in mind, wandering the streets of south central Dublin all night in a daze of despair. What would adored Aunt Bazie say out in Marino, her Armagh pride in my achievement was absolute, or even worse to contemplate, the dismay of her straight-as-a-die husband Maurice, my Kerry stand-in father. He had taken me cycling all over north Dublin's 19th century lanes reading their quaint roadside monuments, or out to Dundrum along the lower slopes of Featherbed Mountain. He made me an Armagh *familiar* to Kerry football, so much so I would fly back to Ireland to join him the day our counties met in a rare final, 1953. His son, my cousin Billy Walsh, I knew what he would say—"you friggin eejit". My vellum fiver was nearly twice his weekly pay with CIE, the national transport combine.

I had intervals resting on summer seats, office steps, a garden wall by a pond which saturated me in dew. At twenty I thought my professional life of two years and a bit was over (again). When two or three women walked briskly past me I realised they were on their way to Mass, so I picked myself up to follow them to a huge neo-classical church on a main road I now think was in Upper Camden Street. More like a pagan Roman temple inside, it had candle shrines to virtually every saint in Christendom. I sought solace from several, heard Mass in my own contemplative silence and decided I could go to Holy Communion. After all, I had by now convinced myself, I was blameless, stupid yes, but no criminal. Not me

There was nothing exceptional in that Catholic Ireland of not so long ago with a hundred or more crowding the altar rails on a weekday morning. The man kneeling in front of me received, blessed himself and rose, turning, to clap a hand over his mouth to stop the Host blowing out of it with the shock of confronting me. For a News Editor this must have been one of the weirdest moments in Leo Walsh's working life. It still is in mine. Three guardian angels, this time ? No, not here, not this time, wrong team. He cannot think anything but that I had somehow cased his home address and followed him to Mass to show him what a good, holy fellow I really was. Neither could he be blamed for thinking that way, albeit most journalists would balk at such a social aberration as a bloody News Editor going to Mass—any day of the week. I never saw Leo Walsh again and I have nothing but the fondest memory of him. My first job on a daily newspaper, my Dublin Evening Mail life, had ended in front of God's altar. Message received and understood. The time for the English boat was drawing near, and I would have to unhook myself from the Irish Press, but not just yet Jesus, if you don't mind, not just yet . . .

"Night Town", was invested with grist rather than glamour, though it could ladle out some of that commodity as well". I'm Night Town reporter on the Irish Press" regaled in Armagh as I swanked homeward in neo-Hollywood garb and swirls of pungent oriental tobacco. It was my counter-punch to school contemporaries who once called me "Big Head" The role playing not dissimilar, the innate glamour of newspaper journalism in its unchallenged heyday, created a public image of a career next only to Hollywood stardom. While salaries would never compare with those in Tinseltown, the rewards for established journalists were well ahead of the exam-entry professions who would not overtake until well into their 'Thirties. In truth, 'Night Town' was a prosaic slog of night-nursing the desk and answering telephones for the Night News Editor. The title was spurious, night-time yes, on the town, no, originated from the trio of American journalists DeValera summoned to launch his party-cum-family-owned paper. The American first touch on the tiller of The Irish Press established a hard news value, outstanding among Ireland's flabby providers of institutionalised news, an edge it retained for all its life. It was broadly comparable to London's Daily Express, the newsman's newspaper in its heyday, in being able to absorb the slanted input of their politicised owners without repelling a wider readership.

All the same, at 19, turning 20 in November 1947, the excitement was mine to savour into glamour. I was thrilled talking to senior reporters out in the country on big stories following a government minister, or anointing a bishop; establishment stories did have precedence in holy, reverent Ireland notwithstanding. Nineteen or twenty, this kiddo from Armagh was in sole charge of the news room when the editor took my night news editor downstairs for a nightcap in The Scotch House

During the law terms of Hilary, Easter and Trinity I lived up to my big brother's judgement of my fiscal behaviour, as he put it in the Irish—*flahule;* I can only spell it phonetically in the English, which still allows it to be *onomatopoetic* in both. So Jimmy thought I was a reckless spendthrift, which indeed seemed to be the case then, but later, with age, much delayed responsibility, I felt able to stretch the translation to mean *generous to a fault*; During the Long (Law) Vacation I was invariably broke and would have been destitute without those Press Sundays. How I spent my lavish earnings in the law terms I now have no idea. Turkish fags were expensive, but I did not drink. I had no girl friend beyond some random squiring a junior nurse from Armagh, her anxious mother had asked Jimmy to ask me if I would be kind enough to look after her in big sinful Dublin and, good enough, he passed on the message, easily done; she was very easy to look at—but mere buddies we remained.

A Saturday night with Mary D in Dublin, 1947: Two grills in The (fairly posh) Green Rooster on O'Connell Street, twelve shillings, two cinema seats, rear stalls or balcony, three shillings, a taxi up the river quays to The Richmond Hospital, four shillings, and I still had the bus money home after very nearly blowing a whole pound. Pause too for a social cameo of sixty years ago. Mary is leaning against the huge tree on the wide greensward in front of the Richmond's main pedestrian entrance. I am standing close beside her, on her left, leaning with my right elbow on the tree, my right hand cupping the side of my head, my left hand gesticulating my chatter all over the place. (It was a very big tree, and might still be there.) Nurse D was garbed from shoulder to shins in the Richmond's thick, heavy Crombie overcoat, a forbidding passion killer had either of us been so minded. Suddenly a huge round flashlight is beamed on us and a deep adult voice behind it says: "What's going on here now?"—I make out an enormous Garda sergeant.

Me, indignantly: "What do you mean, there's nothing going on here. We're friends just talking."

Sergeant: Where are you from boy?"

Me: "I'm from Armagh, why, what's that got to do with it?."

Sgt: "We'll have none of your indecent Northern behaviour down here now. You go on home now and mind your lip, so we'll have no more of this here now, and you miss"—he indicated the gates—"you go on in now before I report you to Matron."

Back home in Armagh, after years of beating the courting couples out of Cemetery Lane with his blackthorn, Monsignor Q was now a bishop in a border diocese. Indeed, dear man, he had, unasked, as a friend of my late father, recommended me to Larry deLacy, editor of The Drogheda Argus, for which much gratitude Bish, because it led me here. The couple-bashing clergy ranting in the pulpit against "company-keeping" made you wonder how they thought couples married or how babies got born, after which both events, preferably in that order, they railed against the sin of stopping them, the babies I mean. The new mothers of Ireland were also "unclean" after having them, whereupon they had to be "churched" before their husbands could start them off again. A wife's refusal to "conjugate" was also a sin.

It took another frightening decade and the epic of the Vanishing Irish—a Harvard professor's tag for it, after half a million had gone,—to persuade the closed, secret Maynooth synods of Ireland's Catholic bishops to end the pulpit tirades against the sin of "company keeping". It was overdue anyway. In west Cork, a year before Garda Sergeant Nightwatch separated me from Mary's overcoat, I witnessed priests staging parish-funding dances in marquees lit by fuel-pressure lanterns. After a few dances, more than half the couples were invariably to be found outside in the coal-dark fields. They were not counting dormice. At the door, their beaming Father-Confessor gave them re-entry tickets One must presume he would hear all about it later, so that would all be alright then.

CHAPTER FOUR

To England—Dear Sam

Mr. Sam McGredy IV
Auckland
New Zealand.

September 2008

Dear Sam,

 As I mentioned on my e-mail, I was a callow youth of 20 in 1948 when I was still law reporting in the Four Courts, Dublin, for the Dublin Evening Mail. After my saintly news editor exploded in the mistaken belief I had accepted a bribe in court to keep the donor's name out of a story, I was sacked. Yes I had your man's fiver, but I had nothing to do with his story. After the shock, and a bad night wandering the city streets, I took it without much more ado because I was bored with civil law reporting, and anyway, still had the backstop of Night Town on the Irish Press.

 As my tainted reputation spread around Dublin's jealous newsrooms, I knew I would have to 'take a powder' as we used to say, and head for England. I applied to a national news agency, based in Shrewsbury, and got the £5 a week job by return of post. My days of salubrious living in Dublin were over but I had the certain feeling that real journalism was coming my way at last. (Bighead throbs again)

 So for the big event, Sam, I lashed out and bought myself a beautiful wrist watch, a time chronograph (it said on the dial) with a rotating bezel—the edge—to set the date. It cost all of two pounds in the Pillar Jewellers, on the corner of Henry Street, just across from The General

Post Office, and then I was off to Armagh to say goodbye to the brother and sister, and to show off to my pals and former companions in always peaceful Railway Street

Walking up the old town once more on a Saturday night I was joined by Billy Weir. I used to play with his younger brother Aubrey. We decided we needed some refreshment before doing anything else, not that we had many options. We stood with others outside Malocca's Ice Cream Parlour savouring newspaper cones of fish and chips, the while scrutinising the dolls passing to and fro. (in Dublin, "de mots", ergo moths as attracted to the lights)). I guessed I would go to the pictures just around the corner in The Cosy Corner and Billy had the same idea. "What time is it Paddy?" he asked. I had already shown him the super watch coming up the street and was delighted with the chance to widen its impact—pleased that Billy wanted to see it again. I grandly tipped up my left wrist under a gentlemanly jerk of my shirt-sleeve. My fish and chips hit the pavement with a squelchy slap . . . Laugh? They roared. Some girls were still sniggering and looking back twenty yards away. A big tall fellow only Billy knew as "Ritchey from Richhill", the village half way to Portadown, was splitting himself. He leaned on the shop window and slapped his thighs as he roared his glee. Disgusted with myself, I slunk off to seek solace in the cinema.

So anyway Sam, that was the Saturday. On Sunday night the Irish Mail, Dun Laoghaire ("Leary") steamer to Holyhead, mail train to London, missed my connection at Crewe. I was stranded all night on that song-writer's railway station. The first train to Shrewsbury on Monday morning got me there after nine and my new boss shook hands with the great news I was just in time for the Divorce Court. Nobody asked me if I had had my breakfast, but I brushed that aside. This was big time for Paddy. I managed to gorb a Mars Bar on the way to the Shire Hall courtroom.

The first thing I noticed in my first English courtroom was the gorgeous young blonde in the press box. After a fleeting smile of welcome, she sat back with her hands in the pockets of a tailored beige cullotte suit, the one with the skirt that's really trousers. It was as if she didn't need to work. She wasn't much bothered, anyway, while I began beavering away with pen and notepad. The evidence was amazing Sam, you never heard the like, ladies petticoats on armchairs, stockings on the floor, a red-haired lady in the bed and a man's shoes under it, all of it evidence from a detective who somehow had been allowed access to this room, or a view through a handy window, and me writing all this down and still didn't know what the Paps were.

About an hour everything suddenly stopped. I looked up and everybody was staring at me. The judge rose and went into his chamber. The Clerk of the Court spoke to the usher, who left and came back with a police constable, who took me by a sleeve down to the cells below. He sat me on a cell bed but left the door open. Only hours in bloody England and I'm in the clink! Just because I'm Irish, right? Perhaps those IRA guys are right, except, hang on, how did they know I'm Irish. I was in such a welter of confusion I did not recognise the Clerk when he joined me, sans wig, until he offered me a cigarette, politely declined by a Balkan Sobranje man. He smiled broadly, followed by a booming laugh as he learned I was just off the boat from Dublin, where of course a divorce court would not exist for another fifty years, something less than that for the North. My crime was very simple. I was seen taking notes, forbidden by law, I heard him say. In a divorce case way back in the 'twenties, a marriage having lasted one day, an unbelievably unaware bride complained of her gentle aristocratic husband's "Hunnish practices" as he tried to make love to her on their honeymoon. The papers, saucy and serious, had a field day at her expense, but no more. Fleeing as far as she could, to the back of beyond, the terribly wounded young lady retired to a life of hunting, shooting and socialising on a small castle estate overlooking Galway Bay. The details in divorce actions in Britain ever since can only be based on the judge's summary. Well Sam, that explained the idle young lady sitting beside me. I was learning England the hard way already.

Leslie Bryce Thomas, my first English employer, was sent for to vouch for me. He contritely accepted a telling off for not introducing me to the court. But he was only letting on, as we used to say, and already thinking of his next story. On our way back to the office he asked : "Do you know anything about flowers?" I told him I knew the difference between a daisy and a daffodil. He was not impressed, insisting: "I don't want results, I want a big story. Shrewsbury Show is going to see off Chelsea and Southport as Britain's greatest, and this is the first one since the war."

And so, on my second day he sent me to cover an event that did not exist in Ireland either, a country for the most part without even a garden culture. Even posh, crumbly run-down Ballsbridge, the faded foreign embassy area of Dublin, was replete with scraggy, pebbly garden frontages of unkempt grass and rusting bicycles. When I related this to the beloved Kerry Uncle Maurice, he said: "Simple, in the long haul after the famine, there was no incentive to make gardens." So come Tuesday Sam, there I was, a hapless, hopeless, spalpeen from Ireland, trying to make sense of this. I spoke to the

British Movietone boys when they arrived in their enormous Humbers, all plus-fours and cigarette holders. Why the cigarette holders?—"keeps the smoke away from the lenses old boy"

Fruitless, in both senses, flowerless, shrubless and storyless, I looked again at my £2 wonder-watch—11.45 a.m—and gave myself a deadline of another fifteen minutes to noonday, to call it a day, my first sortie to England over in two days. I'd be back to the office in a jiffy, resign and apologise "not ready for England", and catch a train in good time for the mail boat back to dear, dirty old Dublin, the city I knew would cosset me again. As my Cinderella moment came I gave the watch a final despairing glance on a weary uplifted arm, but I had nothing to report as we say. I had had my chips this time and no mistake. Back to a scornful Dublin most likely, tail between legs, I turned for the nearest exit.

"I see ye still got thon quare watch ye boy ye."

The shrill, sharp Ulster accent in its Elizabethan syntax rang out as if someone had let off an air raid siren under the big tent. About a dozen others turned to see the source, standing there, his long narrow face grinning at me, bloody Ritchey from Richhill, would you believe, wheeling a long trolly packed with tightly wrapped shrubs

"Ritchey" exclaimed the still dim, ace reporter from Armagh, "what in the name of God are you doing here?"

He straightened his six-foot-plus up to the greater height for expressing the hurtful indignation already visible on his face; "What do you mean what am I doing here?. Sure I work for Sam McGredy, so a do" My own face fell into something like lockjaw, frozen. But my closed horizon suddenly widened. I have always had a razor sharp instinct when the innocent talk of others turns into news, and I have never lost it. He was talking about the world's greatest rose grower and hybridists, spread over fields outside Portadown, barely ten miles from my home in Armagh.

Your family name, Sam, actually your father's name, (indeed, your grandfather's name) hit me like the proverbial ton of bricks. Between the wars no aspiring housewife in the spreading suburbs would regard her home in Britain as complete without a "Sam" or a "Maureen" in pride of place in her garden, ordered by post from the rose fields along Garvaghy Road. You remember, Sam, you told me the firm had hired the meadow on one side of Garvaghy Road from a Portadown business man to extend the nurseries. Sad to say Sam, no road of roses today. It presents a siege to peace in Northern Ireland every year now—just because Orange men and Fenians are arguing the right to march along it, or not, a bitter Protestant-Catholic barricade of dissent since 1995. The Orangemen march to Drumcree Church for an annual service along one road, but their return route, along your former rosefields, houses a small estate of Catholics. They are half a field away from where the Orangemen want to march home, and the Orangemen wont go any other way. Northern Ireland Sam! Wouldn't you think they could catch themselves on! Anyway, your man Ritchey wasn't going to let me get away with my display of ignorance; "D'ye see them roses?" he declared, indicating the barrow, his indignation irrepressible, "Them roses was growing in Portey-down at three o'clock this morning, I'm telling you boy. The boss had them lifted and we took them up to Nuts Corner, the airport, and we flew them here in a big aeroplane, an Avro Anson so it was, he hired from the Royal Air Force to get us to an airfield up the road here. I'm telling ye boy, McGredy's Roses are going to clean up here the morrow"

The hairs on my neck were up Sam, the tingling all round to my tongue I was so near speechless. I felt I'd been hit by the printing spindle on the old staircase back on the Dublin Evening Mail. Sam, and I told you about that too I must remind you here, as you were only a schoolboy in America then, 1948 you might just remember, the Berlin Air Lift was on as Allied Forces in the west tried to stop the Russians throttling the city in the middle of their occupation Zone. Hundreds of aircraft by weeks that turned into months kept the distressed capital in food and freedom. I got the details of this Ulster airlift from Ritchey and ran like the wind from the park they call Shrewsbury Quarry all the way downhill to the office to burst into Bryce Thomas with news copy the like of which he had never experienced himself—and certainly never the like from a bloody flower show. My story was front page in every morning paper, national and regional, throughout the UK. The Daily Express, with its unfailing reach for the patriotic, headlined:

AN AIRLIFT OF ROSES FOR BRITAIN

Bryce Thomas told his £5-a-week reporter (board and lodging £4 10s) "It looks McGarvey, I might lose you to Fleet Street already, and you only here two days" (A faint echo of Leo Walsh and my guardian angels) He'd already had calls from Manchester news desks, and even London was calling him, curious about the sources of the story. The phone was bouncing off the hook all that Wednesday morning. Alan the book keeper held out the handset: "This one's for you." a smirky grin on his face It wasn't Fleet

Street (not yet). It was the beautiful blonde in the press box on Monday, introducing herself, a detail restricted here to J : "Oh hello, we're hearing great things about you. It was you who did it, wasn't it?" She was so warm in praise my head swam (and got bigger). "Weren't they awfully beastly to you in court on Monday ?" We were bound to meet soon, both reporters, she said, but there was a promise of more in her soft melodious English voice.

Ace Paddy got the big story, the gorgeous girl and dig this Sam Daddy owned two newspapers. My Guardian Angel had followed me to Shrewsbury. Day three only—and England lay at my feet.

All thanks to your Portadown roses and my £2 watch from The Pillar Jewellers, and big Richey. So my thanks again for your help and emails, and listen, Sam, I hope they will read this story on Garvaghy Road. Somebody must tell them, live and let live. Perhaps even, a McGredy will grow roses there again some day.

CHAPTER FIVE

Sussex by the Sea

It is August 1949 and I am on my way back to England again, summoned by telegram, to report the trial of John George Haigh, the Acid Bath Killer, at Lewes Assizes.

    The strain on the train was reflected from the rising terrain as suburban London and woodland Surrey gave way to Sussex. The landscapes of *eau de nil* fields, woody copses and coverts, burnt and dry from a long hot summer, faded away to longer views over bare wheat-coloured, treeless hills supporting miles of sheep pasture. An England almost devoid of trees was a complete surprise as the climbing engine huffered and puffered in shortening steamy strokes as the ascent persisted. It looked like America's praries except for the rapid changes of ever rising hillocks across narrow chalk-stripe valleys. A new horizon appeared after almost every mile. This is a well remembered first view of the breathtaking Sussex uplands the English perversely call downs, with their strange aura of unaltered prehistoric times, the hills amazingly made of chalk just like the very blackboard sticks you used at school. Back home such contours would have outcrops of real rocks, limestone and granite. The sheep, whiter than white as in the contemporary adverts for Persil washing powder, with jet black faces, were a breed apart. The shepherds, if that's who they were, barely forty miles from the world's largest city, were in 18th century garb, grown men in decorated knee-length smocks over bulky, baggy trousers, and no sign of concession to the heat. All the windows in the long coach-style carriage were open to allow some breezy relief from the stifling August heat. You might have thought you were in the tropics from the number of men wearing crumpled colonial suits, but weighed that thought against the number, myself among them, still clad in 40oz Bradford broadcloth, the mainstay of the British suit, Irish tweed even thicker. Independent India, barely a year old, was sending the Raj back to Britain in noticeable numbers, to be seen everywhere in the towns they had barely known. The sad looking men in faded Irish colonial linens might easily have thought this was a normal English summer. There were few complaints, or if any one did they were quickly disabused by tales of the terrible winter of two years before when the country froze solid and immobile in January, February and March 1947. For the first time in the 140 years since Britain invented them, the trains stopped.

My rapid English education took a new turn. Huge hoardings abutting the railway showed a train dashing through verdant countryside with the mysterious slogan: YOU ARE NOW ENTERING THE STRONG COUNTRY. The Irish reporter was scornful, well of course Britain was known as "Great" but why brag like this, surely un-English, but the explanation was simple, if not silly.

"Strong" is, was, the eponymous name of the local brewery, and beer, as I eventually discovered, was sold on lines of restricted territorial ownership of "tied" pubs. There were only two "nationals", you could drink in most pubs, Bass, selling India Pale Ale, and Guinness. You had to look around to find bottles of the black Irish stuff, which the first Guinness brewer at Park Royal, London, Lord Iveagh, had persuaded the rivals to accept as a guest brew in their pubs by reserving a considerable chunk of the profits to them. Guinness themselves did not operate pub chains in either country, but in Britain they owned just the one pub, a tiny Norfolk tavern in the Kings's Forest near Thetford, Norfolk, the great manor then owned by Iveagh's grandson, Lord Elveden. A reformer in estate and farm husbandry, it was a hobby pub for him, while keeping a close eye on the brew's notoriously delicate condition at a point of sale. In the years I lived nearby in Suffolk, and a regular for "just the one" when motoring home from Norwich on the A11, it was in the care of a bearded Galway keeper and never anything but resembling the nectar of the gods. It had to be.

Nearly a year of Dublin freelancing in The Four Courts and a renewed stint of sharing desk space with Patrick Kavanagh at The Standard had gone by since I left the WREKIN COUNTRY—and Shropshire's iron-age beer. I had argued my way into Leslie Bryce Thomas sacking me in Shrewsbury because he would not raise my wages from £5 0 a week, board and lodgings £4. 10s. leading to my Micawber-like predicament, solvent only on payday and that was a mirage. Toward the end J was taking me to the pictures.

Bryce Thomas argued I was not earning my keep, yet had hired George Fallows to join me as relief. I then discovered the agency was charging expenses to more than twenty newspapers, on a running murder story, lineage fees apart. For my railway fare to Church Stretton, cash-timed telephone calls and lunch, total £3, his firm collected £60. That was the way the area freelances earned their keep, knowing the dailies in the same group did not cross-check expense accounts (or so they thought). Pipe-smoking George and I developed a taste for Guinness in rural wayside pubs that had special Ministry of Food allocations of real cheddar cheese, a staple of the Shropshire lads, alongside which we usually found the black brew. We presumed someone had decreed the two were as fish and chips to farm-worker energy as well as morale, resulting in bumper crops. Years later, working in Holland for my London Sunday paper, I was frequently slapped on the back and told:

"Holland will never forget that you English fed us for years after the war." It warmed the cockles of my Irish heart, so it did, honestly.

George joined the Mirror some years after I had left it. We had a great re-union on a day I spent there seeing old friends; only weeks later I was shocked by his sudden death in his 'fifties. When a low-or-no pension row broke out on Mirror newspapers in 1968 a realistic group manager, from "up North" Percy Roberts, went over to the City and brought back an Actuary to address us. This expert adviser to insurers on premium against risk told us: "you cant have a pension fund; your average life span is only 51". Not long afterwards my "Man from the Pru" brother Jimmy told me journalists had relinquished their No. 1 position as high-risk life insurance fatalities to doctors. There has to be a moral there as well.

Dublin, still in its "rare oul time" as far as I was concerned, allowed me to return as a "casual", an in-office freelance, in the Irish Press and the Irish Times, on no-court days helping Peter Curry run The Standard, staunch beacon of Ireland's "One True Faith." I was sharing desk space again with Patrick Kavanagh, still the film critic on sufferance, so it was rumoured, from the "chief priest", Archbishop McQuaid. The years ahead would reveal that they were friends on visiting terms to Kavanagh's apartment in Pembroke.

As before Pat would still address me on a Tuesday "Oh man from Armagh, lend half a crown to a poor fellow from Monaghan". The money was always returned on Thursday, and of course I taxed him with this pointless irregularity in his affairs: "You only say that because you're from Armagh and I'm from Monaghan" was his sally in return. When my son

Feargus took me to see the amazing garden-seated memorial on the Grand Canal at Portobello, I sat down beside Patrick, again, and cried. The self-obsessed ignoramus from Armagh sitting beside him in 1947 and 1948 did not know who he really was

Crossing London again on my way to Sussex reminded me of the sortie I made at Fleet Street—my hopeless over ambition—before retreating to Ireland from Shrewsbury. A nice man at the Evening Standard said I was too young. The owner of the South London Press, a reporting agency, upbraided me for a missed appointment and refused another. The junction of Fleet Street and Ludgate Hill was one vast bombsite. The "Black Lubiyanka" as a magazine yet unborn would mock the Daily Express palace of enormous black glazed tiles, stood intact, surviving.

So here I am as the train pulls into Lewes, my first real newspaper job in England, my second English town, the streets visible from the station even steeper than Shrewsbury's. I walked back to the guard's van to collect my trunk and my Gladstone bag, an only heirloom from my father. There was no sign of them.

Somebody had walked them off at a previous station, never to be found again. The shock was devastating, left with no clothes and less than five pounds. The editor of The Sussex Express, Ralph Ravenshear, was sympathetic and promised to make that upstart British Railways "come clean with your clothes"—whatever that meant!

Portly, middle-aged to my 21-year-old eye, he looked more like a country solicitor in his carpeted bow-windowed office, jacket on the back of his chair for Friday morning relaxation, and to show off a comfy home-knitted cardigan, again style and tradition unbowed to any silly old heat wave.

Warning me to be in at 9 a.m. sharp on Monday to be briefed as to what was expected of me in the great trial, he parked me for the weekend in the seaside village of Peacehaven, to lodge in a bachelor bungalow belonging to one of the subs, Eddie. While Eddie shot off to London to do a Saturday shift on a national, I baked on the hard shingle beach watching bass anglers casting their huge rods and lines at a robust incoming tide. Alongside me full length on the stones, lay a strange, beautiful red-haired young lady wearing even more clothes than me, hat and coat, stockings, shoes;; she looked fully rigged for a wedding, drawing stares from strollers

It seemed I had been doubled up as a "minder" of Eddie's ladylove, not quite the right word for the yeoman classes more visible and audible in this part of the country, suspended between the smock-wearing peasantry and the clerical bourgeois. If Eddie was married, she was his "bit on the side". A random visitor to an unattached woman whatever his status at home, was "her fancy man". Even down the years as I tuned into England's class distinctions I never quite placed that girl dressed up to the nines from her hat to her shoes lying on a pebble beach At lunchtime I made an excuse and left her to search for a fish and chip cafe, unable in my parlous state of finance to do the decent thing and bring her along. She was still there when I got back, unmolested in the searing August blare. Some were comparing it to the first August day of The Great War. Back in Eddie's bungalow that evening she did make us a pot of tea, just as Eddie rolled in with a generous bag of the last thing I wanted to eat, fish and chips. That Saturday and Sunday now count as something surreal in my life, long days of not much. Monday was about to put an end to that. As Sergeant Joe Friday used to say in the US TV detective series Dragnet "Just the facts please Ma'am", here are just a few to explain what lay behind my unusual summons by telegram to Lewes for the bizarre Assizes in August from an unresponsive editor to whom I written the previous May. A reporter had gone AWOL in the office car and was found slumped over the wheel in Haymarket W1, more than forty miles away. We never knew what personal demons drove him "up west". He was sacked. By then, the editor of the Daily Mirror, Sylvester Bolam was doing three months in gaol for contempt of court, the paper having named Haigh before Scotland Yard had him arrested and arraigned for trial. Newsrooms all over Fleet Street were treading eggshells around the trial of the century, before it could start, while down in Lewes, The Sussex Express decided it could not make-do with a man short. In the rising crescendo of national excitement, the editor sent for a reporter with the Four Courts, Dublin. on his near-virginal CV. The Daily Express, then the undisputed hard-news totem of all the nationals, presented their pre-trial story under this headline.

IRA GUN GANG TO MURDER TRIAL JUDGE.

Lewes town, according to this flyer, was being scoured street and branch by Special Branch, seeking Irish renegades bent on killing Mr. Justice Travers Humphreys, who had pronounced the death sentence on two of the IRA Coventry bombers in 1938. He was a prosecuting barrister at previous IRA trials going back to 1922.

As the politician says "let me make myself perfectly clear"—the Express looked like a shameless fit-up. It didn't even qualify as Fleet Street flam, the gloss appended to flimsy details to stabilise a doubtful story. No such details existed. But as local police were alerted to the story, there entered, stage south from the coast, into those very streets, an innocent, penniless, blithely over-confident bedraggled young Irishman of no fixed abode, no luggage or identification papers of any kind. Worse, he began to wander around looking forlornly in shop windows, which, to any rookie constable clearly resembled the crime of loitering with intent. He walked green and gullible into the trap. Had I gone straight to the office as the editor had requested as a matter of course, and then the court, I might not have ended up in cells again on this second attempt to "conquer" England. I was in no state to join the staff of a refuse tip, let alone enter one of England's most solemn hanging courtrooms (of which I again had no experience). My underwear was mouldering, my feet steaming in corroded socks. Eddie's bird on the beach had seemed too well dressed, too upmarket we would say now, for me to give her my washing, and anyway, I had no alternative clothes to wear while she might have. Well before nine, the trial starting at ten, I was traipsing up and down the steep main streets in search of a shirt, about all I thought I could afford. I couldn't. The cheapest I could see, all newly invented nylon, all white, all made in Switzerland, and all the rage, was £6, a pound more than a week's wage. Strangely the same shops all offered neckties priced at four pounds ten shillings by Atkinson's Irish Poplin. In bright morning sunlight every shop window on one side of the street threw up a clear reflection of the other side and the two men watching me from a bottle-green Wolseley saloon. At the top of High Street, my shirt safari a shambles, and getting close to the office where I was due at 9 a.m. I turned to face them with the raised eyebrow I had been practising—Mr Cool Me, but hoping they would not detect my stenchy socks, a vaporous incense I could now smell myself. The nails I hammered into my own cell door every time I spoke are clearly visible. The Wolseley had a coat of arms on the door, so not MI5, more likely Special Branch from the county nick. By the way, did I not tell you, sorry, England then had a separate police force for every county and the bigger cities.

What is your name?—Paddy McGarvey

What are you doing here?—I'm a reporter on the local paper.

How long have you been on the paper?—Today, this morning.,

Where have you been until now?—In Dublin

Did I have a passport, sailing ticket ? I did have, but the railway lost it. (they exchanged glances)

Where are you staying?—I don't know yet. The editor is going to tell me today.

What is the editor's name?—er, eh . . . . William Shakespeare

They exchanged beaming glances this time, then one of them took a firm grip of my nearest elbow.—I would have to come along with them, they said.

The police station was further up the street on the opposite side to the Guildhall courts., where I was amazed to see seventeen telephone boxes, unpainted wooden replicas of the red ones, lined up outside. One of the cops told the other he thought reporters were coming from America for this one. As I was led in I brushed shoulders in the fierce spring-loaded double doors against a big burly man with a moustache and dark dank dyed hair, a coarse doppelganger of the film star Clark Gable, Haigh himself, no question. His resemblance to the "King of Hollywood" was reputed to be one his ploys in attracting rich widows in Kensington hotels. His bulk was aggravated by a heavy overcoat, the cold blooded Haigh, no further questions. I doubt if any other reporter would ever get so close—but I had more things to think about. This time I waited in a cell, this time the door open—first day on the job, second trip to England, again.

They could not find anyone at the local paper to confirm my identity. Mister Shakespeare, I was told with heavy irony, aka Mr. Ralph Ravenshear, was delayed in Hastings, where he lived, helping the police with their inquiries into a burglary of his wife's fish and chip shop on Sunday night. The editorial chip shop had no telephone.

They spoke to the company manager, George Martin, who told them—Never heard of him. From Dublin you say, joining this paper? I assure you, that is most unlikely.

In vain, I told them—That's because I was hired by telegram—Where was it?—lost in the train. I was released at noon, with nary an apology from a sheepish Ravenshear when he eventually arrived in Lewes.

He must have been bawled at by the management for the mysterious Dublin telegram, the embarrassment of his wife's chip shop, not quite the thing for an editor of a county weekly, and the shocking calls from the police claiming one of our reporters was in the town cells. The Sussex Express was then owned by Parsons Printing Inks, their tankers of the vital fluid familiar sights in Fleet Street. It was too late to go into the trial that morning. And I never did. A shaken editor briefed me on the rural district I was to develop for the paper, based at Uckfield. I would share an office with Harry. The blot on my escutcheon, as most novelists put it, was obliterated (as they also say) with a staff BSA 250 motorbike all to myself, the use of a shared Austin Swallow in bad weather, and for which he gave me a generous sheaf of petrol coupons, still on wartime rations because of Britain's dearth of dollars. Consolations—and relief, I was not really ready for that trial—flowed over my shoulders like supernatural grace after Confession., A 21-year-old garsun (immature boy, Irish) from Armagh, still not shaving every day, and here I was, single, with a job, a motorbike and a car on the south coast of England, in the longest hottest summer of a century.

Brighton, only nine miles away, was the nearest of a chain of seaside resorts struggling to regain their pre-war eminence for family holidays. Brighton was notorious, again, for its non-family holidaymakers, mostly dirty weekenders. Obviously, as I matured and acquired some wild oats, I would sow them there.

"Did the editor give you any petrol coupons?" was the first thing Harry asked. I handed them over. Harry was older, at least thirty, lean and taller, a Yeoman, and probably ex-Yeoman regiment. Many English counties still had them for this peculiar vanishing class in the country that is still bedevilled by class.

Smirking, he had another question: "I suppose he told you we must use our bikes and to share the car whoever needs it most in bad weather. Eh right Paddy? I said Right Harry. He leaned closer, the more to impart a confidence

"Listen mate, the bikes are for work, rain, shine or shitting bricks, right! The car is for a bit of how're you today Darling. Savvy Savvy Paddy?". And I said Savvy Savvy Harry, although I didn't really.

Savvy savvy, what did that mean, and the other word, was that the same as feckin' in Ireland, and why would you need a car for that? A word that meant something terrible was happening! Surely fecking was the past pluperfect of feckless, so what did this other word mean? My old English master, Brother J.A.B "The Bap" Maloney, would know, surely. Fecking in Ireland meant nothing of itself, a rude-sounding adverb that approved or disapproved of something, mostly the latter as a grammatical derivative of feckless, sometimes as just an intensive. Like for the familiar example—it's the feckin' English again.!

A young journalist was learning quite rapidly that English spoken in England was different from Irish English. Syntax and usage, how you spoke and used the very same words could have a world of difference. When offered coffee or tea while interviewing in a Shropshire household I would say: "No thanks, I'm just after my dinner", my perfectly grammatical Ulster argot brought exchanged glances. They thought I was still looking for my dinner, hint hint, it eventually dawned on me. More than half a lifetime later the Sussex Express celebrated a centenary or similar and invited former staff to contribute a memoir. Mine, brushing shoulders and exchanging a cell with the suave swindler and killer as a putative Irish terrorist, won First Prize, the editor of the time announced—in his case merely a figure of speech, while publishing my account in full, free. Haigh was hanged. I endured another traumatic shock, nothing as horrible, but just as memorable. Lewes puts on a full civic parade and bonfire for November the Fifth commemorating Gunpowder Treason and Plot, the central figure of which is not the hapless Catholic plotter Guy Fawkes, but an effigy of the current Pope. My Orange neighbours in Armagh were horrified. They would never dream of doing anything so uncivil as that. And they don't. Do they?

* * *

Never once in that long ago Sussex summer and autumn of reporting the cricket and the courts did I experience the inside of the Austin Swallow, notwithstanding Harry's lewd leers that my turn for you-know-what was bound to come soon. Harry would be generous, with the caution that I must have my own petrol coupons, which seemed a more onerous precondition than actually finding a girl impressed by a callow Irish youth with a baby Austin; itself hardly a "bird puller". Herbert Austin's pre-war model with a canvas hood and side weather panels looked more like a pram, in a way offering some delayed synergy with Harry's auto adventures. Outside the car my virginity remained intact, not to say pedestrian. The truth was I couldn't drive anyway. In West Cork three years back with chums from Macroom on a clandestine, uninsured trip to Killarney, I was given a brief hairy turn at steering Ray Murphy's mother's new Ford V8 over the brow of the Derrynasaggart Mountains. When my cousin May Walsh in Dublin, Dr. Mary P.J. O'Connor, wife of publican Willy, to her Kerry patients, qualified and became the owner of a Ford Prefect, she gave her brother Billy and me lessons on fabulous, empty, Dollymount Strand. We practised making big speedy circles in the sand and ruined her tyres. That was the sum total of my roadworthiness. I was converse enough with the car's interior, waving Harry off to another assignment for the Express, ho ho ho, to wonder how on earth anyone, meaning any two, could "conjugate" in it. "Conjugate" was a word found in neo-medical books in the "Appliance" shops and slyly by Somerset Maugham. But enough! I was not to think such things, occasions of sin in themselves, warned the genial Irish Christian Brothers who had taken control of all of my schooling since graduating from Mrs. McAvinchey's infants's class on Banbrook Hill at the age of five. At fifteen, sixteen, seventeen, now twenty-one, I was none the wiser

And yet, the upside was, a downy fresh twenty-one-year-old was master of all I was asked to survey for the paper, once Harry had imparted any instructions, a staff motorcycle without the worry of maintenance to be used responsibly for my own pleasure within the limits of petrol rationing. So, as soon as possible I was off down the nine miles to the fleshpots of Brighton to lash out seven bob to see Patty O'Neill's bare breasts in her nude tableaux show. (Well, she sounded Irish, so my lusty thoughts felt entitled)

The Lord Chamberlain's licence for these new shows stipulated the performers must remain perfectly still once the "presentation"—usually a pyramid of chorus girls supporting the star—was visible. My excitement was also visible, as with a start of recognition, I recalled the cautious promise of the Garda sergeant at Macroom that one day I would learn why the twin peaks of the Derrynasaggarts were called The Paps, and me not even married yet.

Not long afterwards Patty married the show's comedian, Alfred Marks, soon to be a national figure with his own BBC programmes. At the celebrity, mostly show business weddings, I would attend later I was never again able to boast I had just spent seven bob to see the bride's "paps". On a much higher plane, I was gravely love-lorn for the lissome blonde back in Shrewsbury. "J" and I had hit it off when I scored national headlines with the "Airlift of Roses for Britain" story. A pal-ship had become a courtship, with some gentle summer-evening kissing in a wide shop doorway near the Severn's town bridge, not "permissive" so much as permission. We were both innocent to a measure unknown now, but she wanted to see me again. Her swain could not afford the train, but the office bike? A terrible temptation arose, and as Oscar Wilde advises, I gave way to it. The temptation included the possibility I might even marry the daughter of a newspaper owner, a thought difficult to avoid, but only of course, my noble spirit arising again, if it was for real love. "J" was an inch taller, in deportment and dress an English Rose with an educational finish superior to mine, headhunted as I was from the fifth form into a law office I was never one for the dumb blondes anyway. Would she click with a strange Ulster fellow who could open Warrenpoint oysters and knew how to address waiters, just a few strands of my exceptional polishing from "P.J"?

Up came a Friday with a weekend relatively free beyond collecting the cricket score sheets which I could postpone to Monday morning, and off I went. Some cricket secretaries agreed to my impassioned pleas to deliver them to the Uckfield office. This was a risky business in Sussex, then one of cricket's premier counties. The game was the first religion of virtually every parish. All that lay between us was a near 200 mile diagonal stretch of an England devoid of by-passes, and baffling cross-roads where the signposts had not been replaced at war's end. One big help—a strong and unerring sense of direction that would serve me all my life.

A pre-dawn Saturday start in September brought me at 8 a.m. to the wide crossroads in the centre of Oxford formed by Broad Street and Cornmarket. The lights were against me and I had moments of deprivation that the buildings around me represented a large gap in my life, beyond my resources to fill. The junction forms the rectangle loosely dubbed St. Giles. The dark rusty stones of Balliol on my right were in shadowed contrast to the sun bursting over the Randolph Hotel on my left. The Fleur de Lys mantelpiece then in the afternoon-tea lounge of that most iconic of English hotels, is now in the front room of Hill House, Hill Street, Lurgan. I put it there, 26 years later. Forty years on I would take perceptive advice on Ireland from a Master of Balliol. who had once been a Liverpool curate . . . The lights across St. Giles turned green and I swept Oxford behind me, better, golden moments in the years to come. The following Monday, having failed to return in time for a morning meeting of a rural district council of which the members were nearly all farmers and titled landowners, I was in deep doodah. I naturally thought a council meeting would meet in the evening. Following my candour and vain apology to a fretting editor, I was sacked for the fourth time in my short career.

Was I worth it? J's parents were delighted to see me, and entertained me royally in a beautiful riverside house at Ironbridge (it had the world's first iron bridge) they were soon vacating for a former monastery. She and I went for dreamy riverside walks on Severn bank, both a year maturer in the big wide world, for long talks and arguments that proved we did not fit the bill for a lifetime partnership. Her father, as kind a putative father-in-law as the amiable, gentlemanly, artisan boiler engineer who did fill that role, took me into his study for a run through scrapbook mementos of his early career. One former motorcyclist talking to this illicit rider, he had tales of touring England throughout the 'Thirties with J's mother in the sidecar while subbing—page editing to newspaper outsiders—the Sunday Express on six pounds a week. That, I still reckon, had been the best of times for British journalists. New printing technology and multi-million circulations had them vying for jobs with salaries higher than those of all the exam-entry professionals. I recall Douglas Brown, a Sunday Telegraph assistant editor in the Seventies, remembering his time as a sub-editor on a Beaverbrook newspaper earning nine pounds a week. "It was 1936, and we had a beautiful Victorian house on Blackheath." The heath was popular with sub-editors for its night trains home. Me, I would make the discovery that pre 1919 houses, older and bigger, were off the wall for the building societies, going cheap as a result. The local authorities, to avoid street decay, would readily lend on them. Our children loved them. They had their own space, often in their own rooms, all seven of them.

CHAPTER SIX

1954 The Sunday Dispatch

Charles Eade, who lived for a time in Charles Dickens's house at Broadstairs, Kent, was appointed editor of The Sunday Dispatch, the companion of The Daily Mail, in 1937. The post was his again by law in 1945, after war service ending as staff adjutant to Lord Louis Mountbatten, the Supreme Commander of Allied Forces in South East Asia. In 1954 he sent for me.

The Daily Mirror had tried a holding ruse to keep me around, switching me from a summer-relief post in the main newsroom to a team for the launch of an entirely new idea, Junior Mirror. It was a separate publication for children. Staffing a children's newspaper with young journalists was a tactical error; some literate uncles and grandmothers might have guaranteed success. Among rivals, only the Express and the Sketch copied the idea, but with in-house pages; the fad lasted about a year. I lasted about two months before being rescued by Eade's invitation. My interview of the author—hero Captain W. E. Johns, did the trick. He was the creator of Biggles, the ace pilot crime-buster and spy catcher, a flying James Bond you could say, with a canvas-wing Sopwith Camel rather than a daft sabre-wielding Aston Martin.

When I was ushered into Eade's oak-panelled office by his affable Danish-origin news editor, Chris Petersen, who had done the head-hunting, a large penny dropped. Not long before, while push-chairing a future Production Editor of the Daily Star across grassy Turnham Green, Chiswick, I espied three men standing close to the Saturday traffic. All wearing suits, one carried a camera, the other a Sunday Dispatch poster announcing the Bath to London Walk, while the third man, dapper in black jacket and the striped trousers—Charles Eade as I would discover—looked more like a sleek provincial solicitor. Even in 1954 he looked out of place and time in an egalitarian town centre. Ever alert for an event, I wheeled eighteen-month old Shane McGarvey nearer to a predecessor of the man he now works for at the Mail on Sunday, just as a thin, exhausted man in shorts and singlet staggered round the back of a bus on to the Green.

Eade extracted from a box, a huge silver cup which he then presented to a badly wilted winner, and the photographer took several pictures.

For all his military and middle-class eclat, Eade's Sunday Dispatch remained the poor relation of Lord Beaverbrook's beacon of middle-England, The Sunday Express. It was the shortage of cash that kept the paper there, employing big stars only when their pull was fading on other papers—Patrick Campbell, Godfrey Wynn, cat-lover essayist Beverley Nicholls. The young third Lord Rothermere, Vere Harmsworth—nickname "Mere"—was taking over as I joined it. Momentarily I created more interest than I merited, merely as a doppelganger to Northcliffe himself, square featured, cow's-lick hair peak, as in the portrait overlooking the front hall, the failed Dublin barrister who with two brothers and their sister Geraldine, founded the Daily Mail dynasty. McGarvey's "Bighead" a favourable thing this time. The Cockney rhyming slang nickname of his great-nephew Vere Harmsworth was a misnomer. When he eventually got hold of David English, previously foot-holding on Hugh Cudlipp's saucy new pin-up weekly, Reveille, followed by the Express, together they would resurrect the Daily Mail back to its newsy origin as a bench marker for Fleet Street. "Foot-holder" was a sub-conscious pun on my memory of David. My occasional street companion; meeting at random he would grab me by the arm to pull me into the gutter, the real one that is, the rain drain, placing one newly-shod foot back on the kerb for my inspection: "What do you think of those Paddy—Six quid in Horne's yesterday, eh?" A shoe fetish, a childhood devoid of shoes? Hardly? And I never quite worked out why he bought shoes in a draper's shop. On the Express he won early promotion to the New York office, which in those years guaranteed a return to an executive post, invariably an assistant editor. Choosing a story in the mid-west in preference to following President Kennedy and his wife Jackie to Dallas in November 1963 he was not in the right place to write the 20th century's biggest US story—but being David, and the Express being the Express, he wrote it as if he was, When he came home, it was to join the Mail where his career would take off yet again.

After listening to Eade's plans for me and the paper, and what we would do together—hiring me as a mere reporter-feature writer—I turned to go and he rose from his desk, as I thought, to usher me out. Silly me, the vain Mountbatten adjutant wanted to illuminate me on his power and authority via about thirty to forty portraits which covered the door-wall of his office. We began on the left side, working our way across, from Charles Eade with Eisenhower to Charles Eade with Pope Pius XII, via CE with Truman, Churchill, Mountbatten of course, at the races with the Aga Khan, deGaulle, Uncle Tom Cobley and all, and we were only at the door, above it CE with our new Queen, on and on over the door and across the back of a drinks cabinet (nothing offered), each one accompanied by a modest little spiel of triumph, especially with Marlene Dietrich, then Bob and Bing, Charlie Chaplin. I was over-extended uttering a train of Oh's and Aah's and My Goodnesses, until suddenly, just before the end, just after the Nizam of Hyderabad, there it was:

Charles Eade with Paddy McGarvey

It was the picture taken on Turnham Green. As I peered over his shoulder;. I said something ordinary like, "Oh my goodness, that's me!" The portrait was cropped just above Shane's head. My new editor's glow of pride froze to a pallor, looking twice again at the picture then back at me, as though there might have been a mistake, or an element of doubt. "Well, well McGarvey, you certainly have arrived, haven't you!" he managed to say, the last two words rising and fading again, an embarrassed falsetto clearly audible.

Now why did I think, walking back down Northcliffe's oak-lined corridors to my new office, that I would be vacating it sooner than I would wish. Brushes with the brush-off began within weeks, the skirmishes before the big one two years later when I went out with a bang over a very swish car, a gorgeous new Jaguar. Two more years wasn't bad though for the time, as newsprint rationing by the dollar eased and more inter-office headhunting began across extra paging.

I thought he "had me" one wet morning a few weeks later. He sent for me before I got my raincoat off. Like the Cavalier child standing before a Cromwellian inquisitor—"Where is your father?" I stood before his huge desk once more as he rounded on me for wearing a corduroy cap, not the usual version but a Breton square-rigged marine design with deeper two-inch side-band and a wider peak, all in a light olive colour for the cloth. How dare I wear such garb while representing his paper? A few years later when the Liverpool Four wore the very same caps over their collarless jackets, I wanted to go back and shake one under his nose. He was no longer there; neither was I. His social judgements were bound by military etiquette and until his own end with the Dispatch dying under him he seemed to think all his readers felt the same. Mine had been worn with a Burberry raincoat, and a grey-blue Prince of Wales check suit, my shoes black Oxfords. For red-letter days of show business interviews, or assisting the social diary column, I set this off with a red buttonhole carnation bought at Liverpool Street Station for a shilling. The Mid-Fifties saw the dying days of British male shabbiness, whether from penury or preference, from pre-teens to pensions; Carnaby Street's revolution was just around the corner and would be much too young in style for old codgers like me, getting on for thirty. But for now, I was easily the best dressed in his office, the while he was barracking me to be always ready to interview the Archbishop of Canterbury. Oddly, the best dressed men in civilian Britain were almost exclusively working class, and went about in string El Dorado ties, white shirts, black frock coats cut forward to the knee, and black suede shoes on two-inch crepe soles, mocked and admired in about equal measure as the Teddy Boys. The "Teds" were a lifestyle unto themselves. They stood out from discharged army officers in mufti, clinging to their army-cut British Warm, an overcoat also cut sharply to the knee, very smart, very short for the time. It was overtaken by the horrible mid-thigh length motor coat, which always creased up on a walker's behind.

Lord Beaverbrook was unapologetic about using his papers to drive favourite causes. His most succesful, and commendable, was the Daily Express campaign to create by law the "skid lid" for motorcyclists. He also loved to pillory the powerful and denigrate his enemies, the biggest in that category, the largest mote in his eye, was the demi-Royal naval hero, Lord Louis Mountbatten. He suspected, with some reason, the great man was ambidextrous in his sex life and just too palsy-walsy with the matinee-idol actor-playwright Noel Coward, who was not in the least ambidextrous. Coward, as with so many homosexuals an inspired genius in his craft, wrote the first great propaganda film of the war, featuring the grim struggle for supplies against Germany's U-Boats in the Battle of the Atlantic. The horrendous shipping losses in lives and tonnage were concealed from the public. A sharply-focused episode of *In Which we Serve* showed a Daily Express front page floating past a group of floundering and drowning British sailors. The headline was clearly visible

THERE WILL BE NO WAR THIS YEAR

You did not have to be a lip-reader in the cinema to see and "hear" one of the sailors mouthing: "F . . . K the Daily Express". The Beaver liked to pre-empt the news as well, you see, especially in public and international affairs. Lord Louis was naval adviser to his pal Noel on the making of the film. Beaverbrook, soon to be an aggressively successful Minister for Munitions in Churchill's coalition, never forgave him, blaming him directly for the public slight on his great newspaper. Limited to what steps he could take in wartime, and Mountbatten's serious jobs in the war, he soon unleashed a peacetime barrage of direct attacks, niggling criticism in social diaries, the defence correspondents in military, air and naval affairs instructed to be diligent in seeking cracks in the glittering post-war career of the CIGS—Chief of the Imperial General Staff, by now Mountbatten of course.

Every niggle, every insult, every definitive defence-affairs article in the three Express newspapers—the upmarket Evening Standard was often employed in the offensive—had to be answered by his lone, embattled torch bearer, Charles Eade. Until he laid down his own baton as editor, he conduced a constant counter campaign and it became a burden to be borne in turn by most of the Dispatch's writers, whatever the event. Our big brother on the floor below, the Daily Mail, was not bothered; it was not a "Northcliffe vendetta" this time, just Eade defending his old CO in the Far East. I am not going to relate any of the skirmishes here because I missed virtually all of it, most likely for the luck, once again, of being Irish.

Outside the withering fire of the Mountbatten wars, the Dispatch continued to battle the Beaverboook Sunday paper by hiring big stars fading from their pinnacles on other papers. In terms of stardom and newspapers salaries by far the biggest fish they caught was Godfrey Winn. The multi-million circulation Sunday Pictorial in the Mirror's stable was built up in the 'thirties by its *enfant extraordinaire* editor, Hugh Cudlip. Aged 22 when he took the post, he was the youngest of three brothers from Wales to become simultaneous editors of national newspapers, a feat they achieved for just ten remarkable days in 1953, Hugh at the Daily Mirror, Percy at the Daily Herald, Reg at the News of the World.

Winn was Hugh's discovery in 1935, worth every penny of his £4000 a year salary at a time when a bank cashier earned £150. Godfrey was a cautious homosexual, driven to the office in his Rolls by his man, Jimmy. He had an instinctive empathy with women, a detached male observer of the legions of devoted feminine readers who followed him from paper to paper as his star rose and declined. Along the same oak-lined Northcliffe corridor I shared with him twenty years later, Godfrey could be quite camp

"Oh Paddy, wherever did you get those divine eyebrows?"

"I got them, in N'orn Ireland Godfrey. Now stop your nonsense, d-hear?"

I was in mocking conversation about Winn with an old friend, Stanley Bonnet, my former chief reporter on The Slough Observer, then on the Mail while writing a history of the Royal Navy. *The Price of Admiralty—Robert Hale* He was coldly disapproving of my attitude. "Next time you see Godfrey, have a look at his hands" I did. Godfrey had no fingernails. I rang Bonnet.

"He isn't the cissy-cum-nancy you all seem to think he is. He lost them from frostbite on Murmansk Convoy—*no braver sailors in the Kings's navee*" Stanley chanted on the phone. He served on the route himself. The dangerous northern sea route to Murmansk, policed by roving u-boats, was the only way the Allies could supply Russia.

For his readers Godfrey could supply sympathy and instant comfort. Here is a sampler from a 1937 book collection of his pieces. It might make your toes curl now, but in those more innocent days his prose sold millions of papers. He is waiting to use a public telephone in a line of four, all occupied, the last by a young girl who dashed in just in front of him, then seemed hesitant, tuppence in hand. Standing outside the telephone box, this is what he wrote about the girl inside it.

"Why is she hesitating? I think I know. She was plucking up courage to ring her lover at his office. She had no word from him for a week, and she was getting into a panic I longed to rap on the door and tell her to keep silent. Nothing is so dead as a love affair that has gone wrong. When that happens no amount of telephone entreaties will bring it back to life. While on the other hand it was quite likely that his silence had no sinister meaning at all. He may have been kept working overtime, or got a filthy cold, or was still recovering from the effects of a bachelor party

And by pursuing him on the telephone, she was not only sacrificing her self-respect, she was jeopardising her future chances of happiness too.

For there is nothing that men hate more than being bothered by their womenfolk during office hours. For us the world of love and the world of business are poles apart

And that is why the eyes of that girl in the call-box as she slipped past me into the street were hurt and humiliated."

His sensitivity to women's problems, and this a classic example, made him a national figure for years before the advent of TV. In my own time I am certain he was the first workaday journalist to feature in advertising endorsements (for ENO's Fruit Salts)

* * *

MOVE OVER, AMBER

In spite of Godfrey's appeal to maidservants and overburdened wives, the circulation faltered again. Expedient help to dam the flow was at hand, from America, where else in those years. Britain was about to be introduced to Amber, where everybody had easily forgotten that she was portrayed on screen in 1947 by Linda Darnell. Cornel Wilde, as her unfortunate true-love, struggled amid a cavalier squadron of others. War-wearied Britain was about to become FAB, Forever Ambered Britain. The author, Kathleen Winsor, claiming direct descent from the Mayfair's Puritans, (surprise, surprise) was married to a college scholarship footballer. Reading his English history notes, she became fascinated by the Restoration period, and began a five-year odyssey of writing, and revision accepted by the first publisher to see it, the august literary upright Macmillan USA. They sold 100,000 in a matter of weeks, millions in home and overseas reprints. Would it do likewise for the Sunday Dispatch a little over a decade after the book? Amber was always sure something terrifically exciting was about to happen—to her.

She was beautiful of course, with a well-cleaved bust now vividly illustrated in her Sunday clinches with lusting cavaliers, from Black Jack Mallard the highwayman to the restoration's Le Roi himself. They never quite went the whole way in steaming paragraphs of panting, caressing, fainting and moaning, as Amber the narrator described the perils and emotions fleeting through her longing, straining body. She would goad another's husband into some perfidy : "Adultery is not a crime, it is an amusement."

More textual than sexual, "nothing" actually happened, nevertheless the book was banned in Boston. (And the Dispatch was banned in Dublin) The attorney general of Massachusetts said it put him to sleep counting seventy references to sexual intercourse, umpteen abortions, bouncing babies from nowhere, and ten descriptions of women undressing in front of men. The sales soared. And now again, so did the Dispatch.

Eade was entitled for a time to think he had Britain by the short and curlies as the well known vulgarity has it; not entirely inapt. His paper was about to introduce an audible change in British argot. *Forever Amber* became a funny and seedy euphemism for hanky panky. The whistling corner boy would exult "Cor I wouldn't mind a bit of Forever Amber wiv that one". All sorts of variations entered the national presumptions of assumed sex. I digress for a moment to tell today's readers complaining of falling newspaper standards, that any comely woman under fifty in a 1950s news story was coaxed to reveal her bust, waist and hip measurement to be bracketed after the first appearance of her name;—*Attractive blonde Mrs. Mary Whoever (36-24-36)*—my toes curl now with embarrassment just thinking about it. The same women would frequently ask Dispatch reporters—What's happening to Amber? Eade insisted on staff coming to a Wednesday morning conference to be briefed with some teasing references to her next encounters, they could relate on their next assignments. Some of us felt like bloody pimps. When Amber had revealed all, Eade quickly bought another book from Winsor to tell more. Sales steadied and then slumped again. One could only go so far; we were more than a decade ahead of a bunch of lewd Australians to be prosecuted in 1971, jailed, fined, deported, the jail sentences later quashed, for producing a school-age magazine called OZ with vulgar cartoons of popular comic strip characters. When the Winsor sagas ceased panting for more readers the man who once lived in Charles Dickens's house felt he had no option but to turn back to the jungle in sheer desperation, with no little peril to his reputation. It would not be the jungle where he had managed the war against Japan alongside Lord Louis.

* * *

And so the new Sunday thrill for British readers came in the loosely draped shape of Lana the Jungle Girl, a female Tarzan. More amazing still, she was a German Tarzan, whereas every British schoolboy knew perfectly well that the real Tarzan was a true-born English nobleman, the lost son of Lord Revelstoke. He grew up in the jungle with an American accent like the actor Johnny Weismuller's, who was, come to think of it, a German. Well, never mind. Lana was barely ever—very barely—seen without her revealing animal skin couture as she swung through the treetops and across the top of two broadsheet feature pages from page four to page five.

We are close to newspaper reality here. One of my Slough Mafia cohorts, Derek Prigent, a senior sub-editor on The Sun, had the extra duty of ringing Rupert Murdoch every night to tell him what his great three—million-plus 'Cash Cow' was leading on, to hear Rupe frequently rasping back at him over pan-oceanic telephone lines—"That's not worth a forest".

Like The Buffs at Waterloo, the circulation steadied. For Mountbatten's *aide de comp* now entrenched once more in the jungle that was Fleet Street, Lana provided some respite. In faraway forests more real trees were felled to provide paper trees for the swinging, writhing, leaping Lana, her adventures lubriciously illustrated in the treetops and below. Writing expenses was the most onerous task on Tuesdays again, with time for bibulous inquests on the previous issue conducted in The Bell, The Tipperary, Auntie's, and the White Swan (local argot—Mucky Duck)—the choice of venue was fairly catholic, provided you didn't need anything to eat. There wasn't anything to eat beyond Mick's Cafe, half way down the Street. Mick featured only one repast, roast beef and two veg, 3s 6d. There were no Wednesday conferences on Lana's future adventures. In those years, working life on a British national Sunday paper presented you with the best of everything. We were masters of the universe. At least on Tuesday and Wednesdays

A likeable, lugubrious Scot, by name Jimmy Reid, was our crime reporter, a job that then required close daily encounters with the Press Room at Scotland Yard. Jimmy took his work as seriously as he took his whisky, a hobby he shared with another gifted Scot, this one on the Daily Mail, Bill McClelland, who did Scottish news-linking duties with us on Saturday. To rejuvenate the Saltire spirit, the pair often shared holiday trips north of the border, made easier by staying only in places distinguished by their names on a bottle, which in Scotland is not very difficult. It was not unknown for them to stay a whole week at one distillery, the better as true cognoscenti, to vet the progress from malting floor to a new pot. Neither were ever seen the worse for wear, in or out of the office. Hardly surprising for two judgmental Scotsmen, their enjoyment lay in the history of a still as much as its taste. They returned from the Highlands and the Isles in much better shape than the two much earlier denizens of Fleet Street who pioneered that route, Johnson and Boswell. In winter Jimmy sported a long black Ulster overcoat under an Anthony Eden hat, dapper in suit and tie. In the summer months he often graced our monastic corridors—only one lady journalist on the floor—in a light frock coat, tailored well down behind the knee, not that you could ever mistake Jimmy for a Ted. He kept telling us, by way of excusing his sartorial superiority—"You must always be ready to interview the Archbishop of Canterbury," Eade's favourite mantra of dress again—to which advice we chorused back—"Why Jimmy, what's he done now?"

One Saturday morning, about three weeks into the Lana saga, Jimmy was advised not to call at the Yard this once, but to proceed instead to

Saville Row Police Station, to assist some officers with their inquiries. Saville Row, where just a few shops share and produce the sublime epitome of British male tailoring, also entailed the headquarters of the West End Vice Squad. The "Tart Chasers"—and dirty book burners—were bored with lifting tranches of prostitutes off the streets, getting them fined in court, and more or less putting them back again. They had been watching and even reading, Lana the Jungle Girl. Not only that, they had obtained a proof page of the morrow's adventure from an easily corrupted compositor; well, what can you do when it's the cops with the bribes.

Lana, they informed Jimmy, is up a gum tree tomorrow, tied high in the branches by hostile natives in the pay of wicked German tomb raiders looking for King Solomon's mines (again). Approaching her near the end of the page where it says Continued Next Week, Order your Copy now at all Good Newsagents, was an enormous gorilla with only one thing in mind (not unlike Amber's lusting Cavaliers, but who were of course, British). Jimmy had to agree that that would be the most likely illustration in the piece tomorrow. Even if it was only a half-wild furry Fraulein who was about to be ravished, he was informed in unmistakable prose, Saville Row would not wear it. There would have to be a prosecution. Younger readers here and now need to be advised that gorillas were always classed in adventurous and even scientific literature from the 18th century well into the 20th as fearsome, vicious monsters. The tide turned quite suddenly in their favour when a small Chicago boy fell into their quarters at the zoo and the huge male moving towards it as the crowds screamed in horror, took protective measures of the child instead of what they expected.

The reports and papers from the amazing American anthropologist, Dian Fossey, sitting among the giant ape families in Rwanda's jungle mountainsides, revealed them as strictly mild, middle-class characters; indeed some gorillas seemed to have stronger family values than most Sunday Dispatch readers. The couples lived quietly, living mostly on salads, the male silverback much like a retired bank manager. The females figuring in TV close-ups liked nothing better from a human visitor than a bunch of flowers—for dessert. The males would eat titbits out of Fossey's hand. The reality always was, if a silverback had found Lana, he would have untied her and carried her down to earth. Fossey, who obtained her degree at Cambridge, was brutally murdered in 1985, the case still unsolved. Few doubt that it was done at the behest of poachers.

But this was gorilla-ignorant mid-century London. "If the gorilla does what the story seems to suggest it's planning to do next week, Jimmy," the

Vice Squad would have to make arrests and prosecute for indecency. That was all that needed to be said. Jimmy left without argument and took a real taxi back to the office, the matter too urgent to wait for one of the big red fourpenny ones. Eade took action before the fictitious gorilla did. Bared no more in surplus lion skins, and spared from City of London magistrates, the unravished Lana vanished, Dispatched you might say . . . its readers swinging in the wind, unable to find Lana facing her fate which might have been much worse than death up there in that gum tree.

It was all too much for the intemperate Randolph Churchill, hapless gambler, failed MP, and roving columnist. He once publicly branded Lord (Esmond) Rothermere, Northcliffe's nephew, who also owned the teasing Daily Sketch, "Pornographer Royal" Excuses were found in the ensuing rows to sack both editors, the Dispatch and Sketch together, in 1959.

Eade's place was taken by a man who sold motor cars, Walter Hayes, an executive of Ford as Public relations manager. A former Mail reporter, he had enlivened a dull motor company by pulling Ford into racing teams beginning with the Anglia's lively 108 engines. Henry Ford, grandson of the original, subsequently made him a board member of Ford of Europe, a successful tail often supporting a failing Detroit dog. Returning to Fleet Street, he enlivened the paper's motoring pages by hiring Colin Chapman, the founder of Lotus, as columnist.

The Dispatch remained a drag on the Mail group's finances and the paper died in 1961, leaving a gap until 1982 when Esmond's son Vere founded the Mail on Sunday. In October 1960, my last London daily, the revered News Chronicle, also died, six months after sacking me for my £17 all-week expenses at Aneurin Bevan's wake and funeral. My former diarist editor John Waddell joined Ford as head of PR and subsequently a Ford Vice President. The wheels go round and round.

CHAPTER SEVEN

In Paris With Gina

By 1956 American cinema chains were reeling towards bankruptcy, rarely more than a third full. The 'Fifties brought rapid territorial spread of the new "cinema" in the home. Television was wrecking business, film rental by the exhibitors sagged as box office sales ebbed away in front of poor movies. It was also causing a noticeable drain on Hollywood's in-house creative talent. What new talent they had they didn't know how to use, for one glaring example, a gorgeous sexy comedienne called Marilyn Monroe, wasted on b-class movies until her second or third "discovery" in Billy Wilder's Some Like it Hot. Even the cowboys were lonesome. They were riding the range, the sheriff's posse still "heading them off at the pass"—in jeeps. The biblical epics which drew the block-long queues, the "blockbusters", were expensive to make, and too frequently flatulent. "Yonder lies the castle of my father the King" said the memorable Tony Curtis with memorable banality . . . Little wonder the uniformed Commissionaires were spieling on the cinema pavements, *Seats in All Parts.* Back home in Armagh, Pat Magee, attired in a peacock blue uniform with gold-braided cap matching anything a South American grand admiral would attempt, lined us up outside the Cosy Corner Cinema in two queues, the threepennys (the thrupennies) and the ninepennys. If the down front ragamuffins became too noisy during the romantic longeurs of the B picture, waiting for Tarzan or Dracula, Pat would hasten down the aisle flashing his torch: "Be quiet there now, this is a melodrama."

Screen sex, sand and sandals had little appeal to millions of teenies and twenty-somethings shaking and swinging in unconnected couples in halls and rooms hired for an hour of frenzy at lunchtime. Rock and

Roll brought scenes of demented office and shop girls stomping and twirling. The boys were slow on this one, the girls rejoicing in this new form of gender independence. In London I accompanied News Chronicle photographer Barnet "Barney" Saidman up to the balcony of Holborn Town Hall's concert hall to get an overview of the lunch-break spectacle below. We retreated rapidly downstairs again from the rancid body scent coming up in unbearable clouds. Just as tights would be reinvented a decade later to cover some terrible gaps under the miniskirt, the body gas from hundreds of prancing girls would soon invent, and not too soon, the portable handbag deodorant, but not yet.

In 1957, Barney and I still covering the rocking frenzy for the News Chronicle, were press guests of the Daily Mirror on their train packed with prizewinning readers to welcome Bill Haley and the Comets at Southampton. It was the first US bodily invasion of Britain by star rockers. The band had been scoring a series of No 1s on the American charts, most notably its trademark hit which British babies were "singing" in their prams, *Rock around the Clock,* its US appeal by then fading, hence the British tour. Generously the Mirror allocated train seats to other papers, a touch of generosity by Editor-in-Chief Hugh Cudlipp. As soon as we settled in on our separate armchairs—the paper had lashed out on a Pullman train—the more sophisticated Saidman spotted that British Rail had removed the silver cutlery and china tableware, replacing them with plain Sheffield metal ware and plebian mugs; surely, Barney coaxed his epicurally green Irish partner, this was a serious social slur on Mirror readers. Nothing ventured, nothing gained, I made my way to a glass-enclosed sub-compartment where Cudlipp was ensconced with the Mirror's editor, Jack Nener

I slid back the glass door and introduced myself, putting the question, did he think it was a slur on the Daily Mirror's readers? The great champion of press license and liberty, the author of *Publish and be Dammed,* in essence the Mirror's philosophy as the champion of the free press, the protector of the weak against the powerful (what more can I say?) replied: "On your way boy, we don't want any smart Alecs here."

I just thought I'd let all my friends know, and my children too, Hugh Cudlipp called me a Smart Alec—and a boy.

The boy to bring both mediums together was Elvis of course "The King". His lustre shone brighter than the biggest stars of the silver screen. In some desperation Hollywood turned to rock and roll in the hope of making him a matinee idol as well. The baby faced Presley was passable enough as a romantic lead, and won new young and older audiences when he took his turn at national service in the Army, which stationed him in Germany.

Territorial expansion of TV in Europe was much slower, caused mainly by state control. As if in free space the European filmmakers, the Italians in particular, stepped into the breach alongside a brief stretch of revived *Film Noir* from the French. They had the weapons to compete with the flickering thing spreading into living rooms. Both weapons were female, of a kind Hollywood had abandoned since the end of the silent era and the advent of sound. One weapon was called Gina Lollobrigida and the other weapon was Sophia Loren.

The social and moral gap, delineated you could say by the Atlantic Ocean, let the Europeans get away with more visible sexuality than Hollywood, saddled also with the strictures of the Hayes Office and the rebukes of the American Catholic Church, at times in uncomfortable alliance with the Southern Baptists. The trick was to flaunt it in comedic situations. Loren, clad only in a straining basque holding up her black stockings (and wearing a hat) awaiting examination by loony Dr. Peter Sellers, makes the point. In today's more tolerant age on sex in the cinema, that scene would have difficulty getting past the censor now, not because of the sex, but Sellers. His stage-Indian doctor would seem racist in terms of audience reaction. Never mind the film, just stick a glamour shot of either on the cinema fronts. Both ladies were box office boffo; La Lollo as the adorable victim heroine men longed to rescue and comfort, La Loren flaunting it as Cleopatra on Tiber—power-sex. Rita Hayworth anyone? Fadeout

So one *louche* as ever Tuesday morning, commencement day for Sunday hacks, mainly to compose their expenses, and I am still on the Dispatch—London's earthier, unkempt newsrooms were rudely wrenched from the ordeals of actually writing their expenses with the warning from their circulation departments that every single paper shop throughout Britain, thousands of them, had received a teasing telegram the day before; *See you at the weekend—Gina*. It wasn't Gina herself of course, it was just Hugh Cudlipp. The *wunderkinde* editor—again, the only man I ever interviewed in a train (by then in his forties) was up to something. It had to be big, but what.?

The ever enthusiastic Danish-origin news editor, Chris Petersen, burst into the newsroom barking orders: "Find her, and the first to do so is on the story, wherever she is" and four hours later I was on my second flight to Paris. The Dane groaned "Oh not you again" but he had promised. he'd promised, in front of seven witnesses, so it was Paddy for Paris again, a previous disaster notwithstanding. I collapsed on the pavement in front of the Bank du Lyon and Mr. Lucky Luciano, stoned, footless, four sheets in the wind at middday after five or six harmless glasses of Pernod administered by the Daily Mail's Paris bureau chief Patrick Murphy who was supposed to be helping me prior to my interview of the most notorious US mafia ganglord in or outside prison. Mid-morning of the noon encounter we all went down to the cafe under the Mail office. Everytime big, elegant Patrick, son of a former ambassador to Czarist Russia, summoned the cafe-maid, he leaned over the bar and gave her a gentle tweak on her left bosom, which set her, and me, giggling. Still laughing as I received every glass, fooled by all that water on top of the "pair-nod." Luciano, dapper in brown English tweeds, smiled across his sin-scarred face as I stepped from my cab, then tried to grab me as my left leg gave way, not once, but twice, and I crashed into the bank wall on the other side of a very wide pavement. That was the end of of my first trip to the City of Light, in darkness. I passed out. Soon afterwards Murphy left the Mail's plum foreign posting for "promotion" as Director of the Daily Mail Ideal Home Exhibition.

Not moving from my desk this time, I rang the Italian Embassy's press attache to ask if their Saturday papers had arrived. Yes of course they had, and so where was Gina, my second question, to be told, sure as all red-blooded Italian diplomats knew, isn't she pictured in nearly all of the papers, departing Rome with her husband, her dresser, her publicity aides, for Paris. She is starring in the big circus epic, *Trapeze,* with two of America's most bankable male stars, Burt Lancaster and Tony Curtis. Simple. Hollywood was about to turn itself inside out with those two Trojan horse jockeys riding shotgun on Europe.

Not so simple was the daft idea someone had conjured up, possibly Eade himself, that I should be armed with a large satchel containing Crown poster sized pictures of the Miss World contestants in their bathing suits, a Dispatch sponsorship which had grown from Blackpool bathing beauties and Mecca Ballrooms . . . It had just been held in Jamaica, and the winner was—the Prime Minister's girlfriend. What a coincidence!!!! Her win brought howls of cruel contempt and charges of "fix" from all the rivals and supporters. And so what was I doing flying to Paris of all places carrying only this huge hard bag of soft porn; I was briefed to ask Lollobrigida, addressing her as the unchallenged, uncrowned queen of moviedom, which of the girls in my pornfolio **she** would have picked as Miss World. This would be a high point of our *tete-a-tete* together in the

George Five, or any other restaurant of her choice. (I told you at the outset of this book I was an exceptional son of the 'oul sod, and so here I am, a gauche Armagh stripling, squiring Hollywood's latest leading lady—such was the plot—in Paris)) To her great credit she flatly refused, but would gladly have dinner with me on Thursday night at the George Five. I did it, I had a date with Gina Lollobrigida. I was so full of myself I felt the need to advise the manager of France's greatest city hotel. He was visibly impressed. As I moved away he began to summon his staff to impart the news.

So, all things considered, I had beforehand to endure the rapt attention of French Customs. Green and Red channels were yet to be invented, everywhere was just customs, no colours, but such was the odd shape and size of my only luggage (The George V always had a supply of paper underpants) I would never have got through a green corridor unchecked. Everybody had to stop and plonk their bags on the table. My man gaped at the first photo he extracted from my satchel. A vulpine leer of appreciation streaked across his face, his moustache stretching right back to his ears. "Henri, Philippe, Gaston" he called out to his confreres—he was obviously a French socialist in these matters, willing to share.—The entire line of them abandoned their charges to feast their eyes on mine. The customs hall echoed to their Gallic Ohs and Ahs, and a recurring Sacre!!! something. The other passengers now visibly stirring, my sinful satchel was quickly handed back with a look of disdainful contempt. I can still recall another moustache curling one side down. Few can sneer with such lowlife dismissal as a French official in uniform.

SCENE ONE: The Royal Palace of Versailles, Paris. The Stables. A decrepit four story building of soot-blackened stone and peeling stucco, the former home and workplace of the Kings's horse—keepers is fronted with large square windows through which the main staircase can be seen. Leading the cameras, lighting and sound crews was the distinguished British director, Carol Reed*, (Odd Man Out, The Third Man) hired by Hecht-Lancaster Productions, Chicago, a Hollywood independent.

*Carol Reed, born 1906, was the son of the legendary actor-manager Sir Henry Beerbohm Tree and his mistress Mary Reed.
The late actor Oliver Reed was his nephew. Sir Carol would win an Oscar in 1968 for his direction of the musical Oliver, behind him lay a respected reputation for his interpretation of the Graham Greene novels.

THE TIME. Early Evening on a cold winter's day. I am standing on Reed's camera dolly beside a man wearing a long black Ulster overcoat under a Homburg hat with a plain grey wool scarf, and wearing light grey kid gloves. I'm trying not to shiver in the light gabardine raincoat in which I left London two days before; a new overcoat would have been going it a bit on Dispatch expenses. I didn't have the time anyway.

Getting here, right here, was one of the greatest flukes of my career. (so far) A scoop in journalism has the same fluke origins as a headed goal. The man beside me, though dressed like an English solicitor in a Cotswold town, except maybe for the kid gloves, was the producer, the American money man who made this make-believe marriage of Hollywood and Rome via France Film, with an iconic London director. Even as a money man he looked out of place here. James Hill was so soft spoken, and beautifully mannered, an American view might have been more accurate to describe him as an upstate, very old style, honest, New England banker.

SCENE TWO. The Director cries LIGHTS—ACTION. Yes really, he did. I heard them. Huge arc lights reveal themselves switching on with audible thumps. In the top window a man is seen peering down; then he begins to descend the staircase, landing by landing, window by window. This is lame, injured circus performer Mike Ribble, aka Burt Lancaster (real previous occupation, trapeze artist) eventually emerges at the street door and exclaims straight to camera "LOLA" The director shouts CUT. Mr. Lancaster beams, then scowls; he has to do it again, and again. During one of the dark interludes, James Hill taps my shoulder: "There's your woman Paddy." There is a sudden gathering of the crews as the new diva of Italian cinema made her entrance, stage left She turned to Hill and smiled. Then Gina Lollobrigida turned to Paddy McGarvey, 87 Railway Street, Armagh, Northern Ireland—and smiled. As our eyes met across the stable yard, my pulsating Irish heart sank like a stone on Warrenpoint beach.

She was much smaller than her front-of-house images, even dowdy looking in spite of a huge mink coat from her neck to her ankles. What brought the shock. was the crude circle of hair curlers ringed around her face from under a Lancome head scarf. *Dinner with this, in Paris.* Would the bloody hotel let me in with a dame in hair curlers? Sadly, that deal was off. I thought someone was having me on. She was awaiting the arrival of her husband, Dr. Skofic. In barely concealed despair I turned to Hill and murmured: "My God, ***she's*** got a long way to catch up on Rita Hayworth."

His brows narrowed in a start of surprise, followed by a wide grin: "Don't worry, you'll see, you'll see."

What I had to see was, we were to dine inside the stables, in a movie-style commissary devised by Michelin guides. At least the food should be good, if only our surroundings were somewhere else. It was not all that different from the studio commissary back in Hollywood, where a carpenter could walk in for a coffee and sit beside Cary Grant. Dinner was free, but Gina didn't want anything. Never mind what I ate, I got an interview through the difficulties of her coping with my high-grade Irish conversation. There were three interruptions.

Burt Lancaster was first. He was also co-producer as the partner in the movie independent company, Hecht-Lancaster. I got a hearty slap on the back; "Hi ya Paddy" followed by "Gina Babe". He stretched across our banquette table to kiss the hand she put out, a gesture that looked like a wary defence.

Next was—Tony Curtis, Italianate in manner and deportment but nee Bernie Schwarz, more athletic and across the table propelled by his left hand on my shoulder to reach her for a mouth-to-mouth classic, short and sweet, her supportive hand on his cheek. Tony also apologised to me. It was nothing original, just the same script. He said "Hi ya Paddy?" muttered a little more simpatico than Lancaster. You notice these things when you dine with the stars.

Filming had finished. The night was getting colder. The royal stables's pre-fab cafe filled up rapidly. A 7th Cavalry charge of some 200 French and Americans, Brits and Italians came swarming in to join us. The noise of those combined races sharing table talk was deafening. I had handicapped myself with a ludicrous bowl of rattatouile and side fries, (no Carlingford oysters for my display of Irish *haut monde*) which I edged aside to concentrate on Hollywood's next queen. Gina's non scripted English was in the grammar primer stage with me limited to some fatuous questions drawing slow, hesitant answers. The barrels of her hair curlers sticking out from the headscarf did not lead us into glamorous chit chat, my usual tactic with the stars back on my home patch in Claridges or The Dorchester. Then Gina and I had the third interruption.

The 15th century stables were not ventilated for a 20th century "caff" with 200 international foodies shouting and masticating at each other. The temperature rose all the way up to join the pall of cigarette fumes gathering under the thirty foot roof, and so did Gina. She stood up to take off her coat, a perfectly sensible thing for a girl dining in mink. The noise fell away to the silence of a Trappist monastery. It was as if Sir Carol had shouted "Cut." Two hundred males—and a few sniffy ladies—turned in sensual unison, mouths ajar under wistful gaze. Underneath the mink, Lollobrigida wore a very thin tangerine sweater, unsupported by anything else, revealing unmistakeably feminine points to view. The silence was palpable in the air, like an invisible ray, and came over my shoulders laden with lust, a laser before its time.(Trapped in between, only 30 inches away from this vision, I just didn't know where to look) My thoughts reeled back (again) to that Macroom Garda sergeant's promise that one day I would learn why those two mountains in the Derrynasaggarts were called The Paps. As ever the gentleman whose Daddy had taught him at age five how to open Carlingford oysters in Warrenpoint, I belatedly leapt to my feet to help her slide the coat from her shoulders, enabling her to sit down again. My action coincided with an audible room-wide sigh of resignation that visibly flurried the pall of nicotine fumes in the roof; she was not for them, not even in her hair curlers. Now sitting on her mink, she was what I had not seen until now, a sensually beautiful woman.

The restaurant resumed the eating and shouting. I was favoured with a kiss on the cheek as I left, her thrilling fingers under my chin. One of the hair rollers gave me a sharp dunt over my right eye. I awoke in the George Five still restless after my most romantic night in Paris. Well, a fellow from Railway Street, Armagh has to make allowances. Head in hands on the satin pillow I gazed up at the baroque ceiling, the deeply flocked wallpaper all around. I padded out to the bathroom to admire myself in the mirror. The roller still left the red imprint. Well, it proved I wasn't dreaming. Hair curlers? Who cared!.

* * *

BUT AFTER GINA, RITA.

England, a lovely Sunday morning and I have a premier left-hand single column front page second lead into a feature page, our millions of readers to enjoy. We ourselves, Pam with her daughter Averill by her earlier marriage, Shane and infant Conal, were enjoying our newly built rented house in Sawbridgeworth, a miracle find in the small milling and malting town tucked into the corner of Hertfordshire that bulges into Essex. It was the country's smallest or second smallest urban district, its rival for the title is, or was, scholastic Eton, and 25 miles from London Liverpool Street terminus on the Great Eastern Railway. Big trains doing the distance, like The Fenman, managed some semblance of express luxury and speed as they rattled the Flemish-style weatherboarding on our tiny little station. The line here is overlooked by the restored country house now owned by the Beckhams. The local commuter trains were still dependant on 1920s rolling stock. The ones you see in old English movies with the slamming single entry compartment doors were just about the end for railway users. What you never saw in the films was the effect of a fatter than average man sitting down heavily in the compartment of his choice with such force as to propel the settled passenger in the next one behind him, to his feet, or as often, in the lap of the lady sitting opposite, a common occurrence when the unique ladies-only compartments were full.

I walked Averill and Shane just the seventy yards or so up Forebury to the new village hall to await the arrival of a touring Redemptorist priest to say Mass for us. On one occasion when he arrived late, he was greeted with indignation by the three-year-old Shane: "It's about time Jesus Christ turned up" Their non-attending Anglican mother had the Sunday morning bliss of listening to the BBC's new folk-music programme from Ireland, led by the plaintive County Armagh voice of a Keady woman called Sara Makem. She sang its theme song, *As I roved out, one May Morning*. Her son Tommy would later be world famous in song with the Clancys. His mother can be found on a Google line as Sara Makem, Ulster Ballad Singer. The programme had origins with friends of my brother Jimmy back in Armagh, and her producer, Professor Sean O'Boyle. It was a remarkable anchoring link to the exiled Irish in Britain. It also rescued the dying English folk music from succumbing to the onslaught of broadcasting pop and rock.

The rest of the day brought more bliss, this time of the temporal kind. My street-of-adventure fame was rising and spreading. A deputy editor rang to say the editor was very pleased with my piece on Gina. Praise from Charles Eade! We had beaten the Sunday Mirror to the draw; they had been unable to reach La Lollo for their project, then hearing she was with me. On an afternoon walk with the children I was treading air. Next door to our house was the larger new home of our landlord's son, Pat Pyle and his wife Jean. Their children John and Ann played with ours, and the houses were separated across front gardens by dwarf walls barely a foot high. The Pyles invited us in for afternoon tea and to see their brand new television set, the first in the avenue. It was an Ekco . . . made locally in Essex. Television had at last escaped the technical confines of London; new masts were going up and brand new ITV in London would soon develop link stations with other private companies in the regions The Sunday programmes had begun about noon so as not to clash with church attendance. ; England was still that kind of country. A news bulletin at 4 PM announced; "*And finally, unexpected glamour at the City Hall Paris this morning when with a special licence the Hollywood film queen Rita Hayworth married James Hill, quiet, virtually unknown film producer. He is now her fifth husband**, Tea with the Pyles would never be the same again. I dropped a bun on their carpet. The shock was such I tripped over the dwarf wall rushing to the phone and nearly fell headlong into my own front door . . . Fleet Street glory? I had been with Hill for three whole days. On that first glance at his star, as he pointed her out, I compared her unfavourably to Hayworth. I remembered his shock, then his grin. He was playing the fiddle—on me. *Sic transit Gloria Mundi*—and watch your back in the office on Tuesday.

* * *

*Edward C. Judson, oilman, Orson Welles (dtr), Prince Aly Khan, horse breeder (dtr) Dick Haymes, crooner.

* * *

THEN AFTER GINA AND RITA, GRETA.

The first and worst fatal crash on the London to Birmingham motorway, Britain's first, occurred a few weeks before it opened in 1959, when the contractor's DeHavilland light passenger plane, chartered to show the new road to county surveyors, collided with a builder's lorry as they tried to land. On an overcast day, working on a virgin road with no route signs in sight I lost my treasured sense of direction and the whereabouts of my News Chronicle staff car and driver, parked under a bridge, but in which direction? With not even Hobson's Choice I plunged across the meadows I still think were in rural Bedfordshire to look for a telephone in a farm or a village. I had to catch a first edition with the story. Nursing a painful stitch and frightened by a herd of prize Red Poll cows merely running to greet me (I was told later), a village green suddenly emerged and I fell gratefully into a phone box. Heaven was on my side, again, the village had a new telephone exchange clearly visible on the other side. I cranked the phone winder and asked the operator to let me have a transfer charge call to London Fleet Street five thousand, my name McGarvey, and the operator replied, "Ach hello Paddy. How're you doing?. How's Jimmy?. I haven't seen him these ages.".

Greta Kelly, from just across our street in Armagh, (and who must have fancied my brother) listened to me dictating copy, then heard me tell the news desk I had lost my driver and she chorused "No you haven't Paddy, I've got him here ringing in." And as I cleared the desk my beautiful staff Humber Pullman rolled up to the box. Yes, you could call that the luck of the Irish.

CHAPTER EIGHT

A Mirror to Ireland.

Between the breaks from fierce and fun-filled work cross East Anglia for The Sunday Mirror. (how about three Norfolk brothers marrying three sisters. Ok, find three white Daimler Sovereigns for the weddings, my news desk commanded) I was briefed in secrecy on the Mirror group's worst kept secret—to establish and print local Irish editions in Ireland using facsimile pages composed in Manchester, As the pet Mick who could deal with the natives, I was engaged to gauge the interest of local editors and correspondents throughout Ireland. Company expenses made for frequent visits to my family home in Railway Street, Armagh, still occupied by my brother Jimmy and his wife Peggy. Nuala had married John Fox of Killybracken, who with his family, were producers of wonderful fluffy floury white potatoes on their steading near Dungannon, in Co. Tyrone. My sister was missed, from Armagh, that is. Two doors away Mrs. Cassie McDermott bewailed: "a wee angel has left Railway Street." The wee angel is average height for Irish ladies; Cassie, God rest her, mother of Maura, Nettie my assigned childhood sweetheart, John and Siobain, was noticeably taller than her husband John Joe, who when I was six, held my hand and walked me across the city behind my mother's hearse.

Jimmy was still declining promotion in the mighty Prudential which would have taken him away from Armagh, the thought of commuting 19 miles to Newry the end of the earth for him. Peggy McGarvey was a Curran, her father Paul the manager of the family Curran Theatre Chain's picture house in Newry. The Curran group sold their thirteen cinemas to the Rank organisation in the mid-'Fifties for a reputed £2m, a deft move in timing just ahead of the TV-induced slump in movie goers. Peggy was a PE teacher in Sacred Heart Convent, Armagh, duly the mother of Fionnuala and Maura, their son Seamus as yet unborn so Hollywood would wait a little longer for a Curran Theatres grandson to sustain another cinema revival as the renowned director of cine photography he now is. It was Jimmy's elder daughter who reawakened my memories of infancy with my mother. Fionnuala, now a Florida housewife, is her generic doppelganger, in colours and style, but the way genes cross families, it is the dark haired Maura, also married in Florida, who walks and talks like my bonde mother. When a family of American cousins saw Seamus at the Oscar ceremony (nominated for the film Atonement) they exclaimed, "Hey, he's a Mullaly"

On my first day on the Daily Mirror in 1954 the deputy Night News Editor, John Theobald asked me to tone down my story on the girl lost in the North Sea from a Harwich steamship. "McGarvey I fear you will make our readers cry."

Theobald was a founder tutor of the Mirror's school of journalism at Plymouth, the one exotic Mirror fancy the rest of Fleet Street chose not to follow. He coached into journalism the young, footloose, bag-piping writer Alastair Campbell, a man who would make many readers tear their hair when he was a Downing Street policy wonk. I resisted a rejoinder to Theobald that readers's tears was the whole idea, and obediently complied with a subdued rewrite. For fear of doing anything similar here, or more likely causing my readers to weep, the childhood story of the very young orphaned McGarveys is best told in thin dry slices. Photographs of Jimmy aged seven and eight show an unsmiling boy. Among the host of very young children playing in the gardens of May Terrace in Railway Street, he alone knew his mother was seriously ill. The devil-may-care, laughing braggart of a brother had nary a worry in the world until she suddenly left us in 1934, aged 37.

Nuala appears in rare photos aged two on my father's cradling arm. Granny Mullaly died three years later in 1937, my father in 1942, leaving Jimmy 18, me 14, Nuala 10, officially orphaned. And yet, I look back on a happy childhood thanks in very large part to the other children tolerating me alongside, the McDermotts and their first cousins, the O'Reillys, the Beattys, Teevans, Forsters, McCutcheons and Lynases. A tall slender boy in long trousers came walking through our territory from another part of town. We rated him "O.K" because Kevin Keenan was visiting his uncle, the Railway Street grocer Barney Fox. Mr. Fox was very popular, not least for delivering small orders on a little cart pulled by a Shetland pony, trotting along with half a pound of butter, a pied pony accompanied by a chorus of delighted children Keenan, at a later stage, would become a friend for life, as did Nuala, yet another displaced O'Donnell from that royal family he found way down in Tipperary for his wife. Kevin got a job for life, would rise to the top, a confidante of the owning family. Most of us would emigrate to find work. In his case the firm came to him, the mighty Mac, Sir Robert McAlpine, building a milk-dehydration factory a few miles from Armagh, and were impressed enough to invite him to go back with them. He went. We were all of an age in a mixed peaceful street.

Living in a small house opposite the grand Italianate railway station, a family with a rather lumpen boy of two moved away to the country near Hamiltonsbawn, still beside the railway. The slate roof of the Paisleys's new home carried a fleeting white-paint warning to passing passengers—Prepare to Meet thy God. Many, laughing nervously, would whip down the carriage window to get a better look, sometimes followed by another nervous laugh. The same stretch of line had seen Ireland's worst train disaster, still in local memories from 1889 when sixty died and 269 were injured, most of them quite young children on a Methodist church excursion to the seaside. The preaching Paisleys moved back to Armagh when Ian was eight. His father was a well-liked drapery assistant in Lennox's Department Store. Down the years of terrorist turmoil, so often marked and sparked by his scalding wounding words in all directions, the grown-up Railway Street children wondered if Northern Ireland's sad history would have been kinder if he had stayed with us. : In the wishful wisdom of hindsight, most of us liked to think so.

The young McGarveys nearly left each other in 1942; Jimmy to move into family-friend lodgings until he could support himself. I was earmarked for despatch to a Dublin school for the orphaned sons of gentlefolk, The O'Brien Institute, not to be compared in any aspect with nearby Artane Boys Institution, reserved for the city's common tearaways. Nuala was to be "adopted" by beloved Aunt Bazie Walsh in Dublin, As for me, I had a lucky escape. The O'Brien was actually a flogger's academy, Artane the decent place by any real comparison.

My mother's sister, real name Elizabeth, raven-haired to Ada's blonde, married to her Kerryman Maurice Walsh, who called her Lil, was the generous, motherly, uncomplaining hostess of our boisterous summer holidays in Marino, next to Clontarf-by-the-Sea, our route to the children's paradise some angelic being had named Dollymount Strand. "Bazie," was her lifelong nickname from her birthname, Elizabeth, explained by the guess that she was dyslexic, the spelling of the nickname part-visible in her proper name, backwards. My daughter Fiona Elizabeth, strongly resembling her, is also dyslexic, but her attempted infant reversal of that, Oofa Bif, did not stick. Sadly Aunt Bazie had lost a little girl, Norah, so my sister Nuala would come as a Godsend. Baby Norah Walsh, named after a Kerry grand chatelaine to Acres Farm in Kerry, was swept away with many other children in a diphtheria plague that smote Dublin in the 'thirties.

Nuala stayed very happily there with her cousins for a little while after Granny died, until my father's politely insistent letters, pleading for her return, brought her back to Armagh. Dame Fortune was on our side, Nuala's especially. This time, a physically handicapped girl of 20 "just in from the country" with her family and now a neighbour just across the street, was waiting to guide and chaperone her for all the years it took to mature from pre-teens to a much loved and admired gentlewoman. Kitty Hagan firmly appointed herself our housekeeper-cum-Nanny after the older Hagan sister Nan my father had hired, left to work in a Bangor summer-season hotel where the marriage stakes for maidservants were easier (and she married tall, handsome easy going Mick Callaghan). So Kitty became our ten-shillings-a week treasure, keeping the wage in her family; she slept at home, just adult enough to keep us in line and together; chatelaine, cook, neighbour, companion, friend. Even when married to Tommy Burns, a billiard table impresario in the mining camps of Australia (and a marriage of tender empathy, Tommy wore a surgical boot) she remained in constant interchange with her young charges for the rest of her life.

Kitty lost her leg by amputation after breaking it in a fall from a wall. The plaster was retained too long in the county infirmary causing gangerene. Outwardly, the loss rarely revealed itself. She dressed normally and modestly in frocks and skirts, never slacks, her hemline just covering the flexible joint of a bespoke Roehampton leg. Johnny Hagan, her father, as a carpenter frequently off work, somehow managed to acquire it from the rehabilitation Surrey hospital for the unreachable 1930s sum of £80. Perhaps the hospital trustees helped. His middle daughter was worth every penny. "Our Kitty" was wise beyond her years; she spoke evenly and gently in perfect grammar (as did her mother), knew instinctively right and wrong in behaviour and dress. Jimmy, 18, resented "being ordered about" but for all his grumbling, we three were lucky, in our Kitty.

Railway Street is still on the edge of the town, forking to Moy Road and Loughgall Road. Two grocer-garages have arrested the decline in residence at the end, and a surprising branch of Marks & Spencer adding some lustre, style even. Noticing a busty rural hoyden striding past with her glass-jar radio battery for charge exchange, in a too-short summer dress, the garrison town packed with Allied troops from western Europe and north America, Kitty harrumphed at me: "*Will you look at the cut of that one, parading up the town in her figure.*" Reading in the corner of the front bay window, I determined to put that in a book some day.

Jimmy and I teased her unmercifully about her one and only problem with spoken syntax: Kitty thought the word cheese was the plural of a chee. Food-picky Jimmy was indifferent to the stuff even its meagre wartime rations; Kitty would scold him: "Eat up that chee"

To make all this possible though, there had to be something else and someone else. We had both in spades. It came from two men, one, a great buddy of my father, "J.P". MacRory,—"J.P and P.J"—and the other, his second cousin, Gerry Lennon (his father James and P.J were cousins). He was a solicitor with a wide reputation as a trial lawyer, a witty defender of even the most miserable petty thieves before delighted RMs* of Petty Sessions, who loved having him in their courts; the former, "J.P" was often referred to by my father as "Wee Joe", as in "Wee Joe wants me" and he would be off like a shot because "Wee Joe" was Cardinal Prince of Holy Church, Primate of All Ireland

*Resident Magistrates, salaried local judges.

Our house in Railway Street, No. 25, since changed to 87, was allocated to my parents as a wedding present from Granny Mullaly, not only retaining ownership, she came along too, my father accepting with good grace a nearly new house with a built-in mother-in-law. It was one of several properties the prison-warder-ex-soldier's widow owned in the street. I have worked out the source of her wealth as the only child and heiress of a well-run Presbyterian farm in Offaly, forgiven even for marrying out and converting to Rome—all for a landless Dublin Fusilier from a struggling Kildare farm of brothers at Ballymore Eustace . . . A year before her death in 1937 she disposed of three other rented houses across the street to a near neighbour, Johnny Cauldwell, as well as the largest house in May Terrace to the McDermotts, enabling them to leapfrog from the smaller house beside us to their huge new home two doors away. At one of her regular Thursday afternoon Buckfast Tonic Wine soirees, I heard her tell the ladies: "£400. that's all I asked for it. I sold it cheaply because I'm very fond of John Joe, such a nice man" (he was also a very handsome man, doubtless another price reducer). When her will was read, shock horror, she had left £300 War Loan bonds and the title deeds of No 25 to Ada, my mother, dead three years before, but had not amended the bequest. Since her daughter's death, a convert brimming with Catholic zeal, she had made one pilgrimage to Rome to see Pope Pius XI. She followed that trip a year later with an eventful journey to America to visit her three sons, Leo and newly-wed Myles, only to find that her eldest, the beloved John, a Jesuit, had fallen out with a bishop, had laicised himself and was illicitly married to a charming Southern Belle teacher in the military academy where he was chaplain. The Mullaly family dramas continued. The college retained him as a teacher; he eventually became headmaster. His shattered mother, after failing to get solace from an unhelpful Cardinal Spellman in New York, from where he had no jurisdiction, came home to a likely earlier death than might have been. From her Rome trip she brought me a wooden whistle painted in Italian national colours. Disgusted, I gave it to a boy on Banbrook Hill I presumed to be even poorer than me.

In Ireland the legal moves to validate her will required two independent citizens to appeal to Chancery to verify my father as a disinterested custodian of his children's estate, inherited on our mother's death, and that's what happened; I have seen the papers in the Ulster Record office. When my father died the house came to us with a £300 charge, debt, mortgage, whatever, its origin not detailed, but most likely the totals of costs incurred in sending my mother to a Swiss clinic, flying there and back. In an open-cockpit plane piloted by "Dick" Hearn, whose mother was a former headmistress of Banbrook Parish School, she flew from Baldonnel, Dublin, to Hendon, London, and from there, or perhaps Croydon, to Zurich by Imperial Airways. The long leather coat and matching fur-trimmed bonnet for the Hendon flights survived for years in Dublin until her sister Bazie's ageing frame could no longer accept the coat.

The medical belief in cold night air as a possible cure for TB was universal. Patients everywhere were pushed out onto sanatorium verandas for the night. The mountain Alpine air failed. As a cure the night air failed everywhere. In the love and mounting fear of losing her, someone suggested a Mediterranean cruise. The hot dry air of a month in Morroco might work the miracle. She went out on a cruise liner from Dublin, returning on another.

She could never have looked better, and I can see her still. Jimmy and I had no warning, Nuala still a babe in the pram. The return of the council chairman's wife from Africa sent a ripple of astonished curiosity throughout the cathedral city. They would have marvelled and gaped—and laughed—more had they seen it happen. I was perched precariously on the "big lav" in the back yard, straining to generate a No 2 with a cut square of the Irish Independent ready to hand when she suddenly appeared round the scullery corner, a dreamy vision in a pale brown linen suit with enormous white buttons. Her blouse had a wide lace collar draping squarely over her shoulders, her hair pulled back into a Heidi bun emphasising the tan she had acquired in Morocco. My mother resembled nothing so much as a contemporary film star, a memory retained by her film-mad son interviewing actresses in the years to come. I was five. She was 36 in 1933, with barely a year left, so that this cameo forms the last sweet memory I can muster of the flash-tempered girl who was my mother, the earlier ones fraught with my bad behaviour and her ailing, shortening moods. Always athletic, she hunkered down to me proffering an enormous cardboard box which a beaming railway porter had just carried from the station for her.

"Look Paddy, look what I brought you from Africa".

What she brought me from Africa gave me such a shock I let go the edge of the lavatory and fell into it. This might have been my last time in her arms as she pulled me up again, not averse to a burst of laughter at her silly son. The live, full-grown tortoise in the box took Armagh by storm for a whole week, the like of it never seen in the city before. A queue formed at the front door, while many unaccompanied children came round the back to peek into the garden from Geordie O'Brien's Field. The tale of Timmy the Armagh tortoise ended in tragedy a week later. A neighbour from Banbrook Hill, Eddie Branken, my age, brought his dog to see the tortoise as well. The big Lurcher took one look, and snapped poor Timmy's head off.

The City of Armagh, its municipal council prorogued by Stormont the following year, 1934, closed down shops and offices for P.J's wife as her winding cortege of over a hundred mourners made its long march from the isolated rural sanatorium beyond the city boundary and in through the narrow shopping streets encircling St. Patrick's Church of Ireland Cathedral, to lay her in St. Patrick's Catholic Cathedral. I marched all the way, nearly three miles, Maura and Netty's Daddy holding my hand. Jimmy was in front of us with my father. At the city centre a man behind us murmured: "Look John Joe, Lennox's have drawn the blinds". The huge windows of the department store were all blanked out. The Lennox family supported the Paisleys, is the way it was seen, and Ian's father worked there.

John Joe said : "Oh, decent people, decent people.!"

The memory of that day faded and stayed away from me, completely locked from my mind, until November 1963 and the shock of seeing the infant John Kennedy standing beside his mother at his slain father's funeral. JFK's tragic only son was wearing my pale dress coat, same velvet collar, same shoes, but not the uncomfortable "pull-ups" I wore below, button-up leggings held in place by a foot strap. The anguish of their day brought mine flooding back. I found I could again recall the nightmares, waking up screaming. I had been running away from her as usual, nothing as bad as the real shin kicking and yelling as she dragged me up to Banbrook School. Her bad-boy in the dream was refusing to come in for bedtime again and she was flying after me, holding her long tea-dress (changed into every day at four) hoiked up above her knees. I am yelling. She is laughing, and then her hand is on my shoulder as she catches me. I turn round to be grabbed in her arms, and she is not there. There is no one there.

I wake to hear Granny Mullaly wailing: "Is there no one to stop that child gerning all night?" Counselling for a grieving child? Therapy? Not anywhere in 1934. Eventually, there was relief, indeed a stroke of genius. Someone had the desperate idea to move me to the Beattys's house four doors away. My soulmate of all childhood, Georgie had been elevated to a new bed and I was allocated his cot, in his room. Beside him, I would become the Deputy-Commander of Railway Street but unlike the claim of another deputy-commander in the years ahead, a real commander was quite visible. Georgie, handsome but with the bulldog glare, he could have passed for Winston Churchill at eight. The nightmares were no more. Aunt Bazie: ever the story teller, she loved telling her visitors in my presence, during my twenties, her eyes and mouth creased in suppressed glee: "We put him in a Protestant cot and that shut him up"

Cardinal MacRory, waiting at his Cathedral, was still on the primatial throne when my father died in 1942, three years to go for himself. He lifted the £300 debt off the house and put it in a desk drawer, where it remained until 1955. His successor, Cardinal John D'Alton, handed it to the Prudential Assurance Company's most successful agent throughout the UK, his close friend and erstwhile press agent: "Here Jimmy, I think it's time you took charge of this."

* * *

MY LIFE AFTER EDDIE'S DOG.

Thirty four years later I am labouring in Final Finish, a toiler in one of Vauxhall Motors's two daytime production lines in Luton. It is November

1967 and I have just turned 40, working secretly, undergound so to speak, I am putting the finishing touches to Vivas, Victors and Crestas. The Vauxhall Victor Mark Two had revived the company market share after the slump that followed Harold Wilson's 1966 "July Squeeze" and his adroit attempt to save bankrupt Britain by devaluing the pound. Fly-boy Harold told us the international pound was not the same as "the pound in your pocket," a claim met with national jeers. Concealing my delicate lilywhite hands as much as possible, I was a secret ringer from the Sunday Telegraph studying the chaotic motor industry from the inside. I had been on a Telegraph salary while trying to get in for nearly seven months when I was finally swept in at last on the Victor Mark Two's waves of recruitment. This was a position of no little danger if discovered at the works end, severe embarrassment for the paper if found out at the top end.

Suddenly, another group of newcomers came along the line with a foreman dropping them where needed. A spare little guy with cropped red hair and one gold earring was parked on the other side of the Viva I was finishing and roared:

"Holy mother of God Paddy McGarvey—Eddie Branken Paddy, God Paddy, do you mind thon tortoise?!"

The Brankens moved away soon after Eddie's big lurcher hound ended Armagh's tortoise odyssy in one bite. Armagh's first and only African immigrant died to a chorus of many children crying. The feat of Eddie's recognition of me since age five to forty was of less import than the stomach-churning fear of what else he might say, but he had no knowledge of my real occupation. And after a few tense exchanges he vanished into the maw of the factory. I never saw him again, even though I would survive three months as a British Stakhannanite. Was ever so small an animal remembered for so long?—but wait.

Sixty years on, 1994 and newly settling again in Armagh, I am walking in Cathedral Road when a tall man stoops out from the small doorway to his little terrace house beside the Parochial Hall and exclaims. "My God, Paddy McGarvey. Well I'll be jiggered. Man dear, Paddy, do you mind thon poor wee tortoise?"

"Spud" Murphy was the childhood survivor of a horrifying accident only yards from his present doorway when a group of young children returning from school tried to play "swings" on a wire left hanging to street level between two poles. It was a live cable. Five were killed, including two Murphy brothers. That dreadful accident has been completely forgotten in Armagh. No one had forgotten my tortoise

* * *

A STATELY INTERLUDE.

Gerry Pagano, who, with his Norwegian wife Bjorck, made me the proud Godfather of their children, Margareta, Kristin and Erik, was one of the News Chronicle's more artistic photographers, his work often in exhibitions. Freelancing later from his home near Saffron Walden, Essex, he got a call to photograph his local MP, the statesman R.A. "Rab" Butler, and his (second) wife-to-be, the widow Mrs. Mollie Courtauld, who knew Gerry. She asked him: "Which paper are you representing today Mr. Pagano?"

"The Guardian, Miss Courtauld", Gerry responded.

"The Guardian Mr. Pagano! "the future Lady Butler exclaimed. "The Guardian is not a newspaper Mr. Pagano. The Daily Telegraph is a newspaper. The Daily Telegraph prints the news. The Guardian merely prints the isms." Gerry took some charming shots anyway of the newly engaged couple and one of them duly appeared on the front page of The Ism.

CHAPTER NINE

A Bad Confession

On the Sunday Mirror, its chief correspondent across East Anglia, the family in a blissful town house in ancient Bury St. Edmunds, where Cardinal Stephen Langton and a few monks wrote Magna Carta about 800 years ago, I was jousting now for parliament, and by the unexpected invitation of people in the counties Tyrone and Derry to fight Mid Ulster, one of Northern Ireland's eleven seats in the House of Commons. (it now has seventeen). I lost the nomination for Armagh to Don Ewart, the election agent to one of Labour's giants, the Coventry MP Richard Crossman. Don, born in the Armagh weaving village of Bessbrook, was also a future Lord Mayor of Coventry, a post with a world-wide dimension, and all those years later I told him so. After the tumult of my selection in Omagh I decided I had to gird my spiritual loins, cleanse my soul and clear my mind to prepare for the battle ahead, a simple exercise available in any part of Ireland on any Saturday morning throughout the year, in those years anyway.

Across Ireland's green fields and blue mountainsides of some saints and too many scholars, thousands of priests were sitting in small wooden cabins waiting for people to kneel beside them in semi—anonymity, sifting sins face-to-face through a sheet of fine metal gauze, before administering a mostly mild reproach mixed with a little praise for future promise. I went to Confession. There was always a two-way contract in this holy sacrament which thanks to the stupefying blunders of the council Vatican Two, has been virtually swept away in favour of a catch-all Confiteor said in monotones at Mass. Aside from God of course; you chose the priest, his name over the door, because you liked his tone and his terms, while he in turn pretended not to know who you were. "*It's easy speaking with Father Green*" the false promise to the Croppy Boy in that same-name song, the priest an army officer in guise seeking rebels, nevertheless explains the custom and the sacrament. And so off to Armagh with me, vile sinner!! But only because I had family to call on as well.

St. Malachy's Church was on very familiar ground. It still to this day looks brand new, replacing the crumbling old pre-Emancipation church in Chapel Lane. Passing to and from school at Christian Brothers, Greenpark, I watched it being built as a chapel-of-ease to Ireland's unrecognised national cathedral, where I was baptised at the age of two hours or so. In tribute to the 12th century monk and bishop, its style is a simplified Irish monastic, with stones from local quarries hewn by local masons, all under the eyes of two Armagh master builders, the brothers Tommy and Hugh McKenna. It was a bulwark of the church in Ireland to find men in small towns able to build churches from local stones and imported marble. St. Malachy's stands only yards from the house where the saint was born, just a little further away than its predecessor was, on land behind his house. An earlier chapel of his time might have been built in his back garden. Is there any other church in Christendom to claim such synergy with its surrounds? Well, yes of course there is, but Bethlehem doesn't really count, an obvious fix by the Master Builder. In 1994, when I returned for the third time on a peace mission, in my native city it was the only church in which I could find solace. The cathedral's Vatican Two's council makeover Mass with alterations for all was a scenic mess denounced by one distinguished (English Catholic) columnist in The Spectator. I think it was me who thought the sanctuary resembled "the Temple of Ra". It had to be done over again, not least because I had dared simultaneously to write the same critique for rival Belfast papers. I was responding to the gritty, suppressed complaints of school contemporaries, the most foolish behaviour imaginable for a returned expatriate.

My rebukes were thrown back in my face, I was the writer and it was up to me to rouse the faithful. It was never put quite like that, but I had my own level of anger. A glorious Italianate pulpit of white marble and gilt, its business edge rimmed under scarlet velvet had been torn away to be replaced by an enormous crucifix on which God made Man more resembled a tree split by lightning, craft taking over from art. The second attempt presents us with something resembling a Busby Berkeley sound and dance stage. St. Malachy's in contrast to the muddled cathedral inside and out, still looks like a Catholic Church. It was spared the universal turntable redecorations because of its wide narrow Sanctuary, leaving it intact with its side altars; only the central one was moved forward to permit the priest to stand with his back to God. My faith was anchored and retained by it. Back then in 1964 a priest who in his early years was a Saturday counsellor to my teenage years, "wee Father McKee" carefully avoided my troubled awakening to the mysteries of sex, the simple, straightforward explanations withheld from all of us by pastors, teachers, and if you had them, silent parents. By now he was in the top tier at Armagh, Administrator. He would be my real Father Green. So I had no "pother" telling him of my injustices to my children, cheating on my expenses, and still lusting after my onetime dinner-in-Paris companion, Ms Gina Lollobrigida (I left out that she was in head-scarf and hair curlers, hardly even an occasion of sin).

Three Hail Marys and one Glory Be To the Father later, successfully lighting my usual post-confessional fag—a "Nelson"—in front of the church in spite of the stiff breeze and basking in a state of supernatural grace, which can often be confused with an overweening self-confidence, I began to hear voices on the wind calling me, calling me, getting louder and closer, "Paddy, Paddy", turned, and there was Father McKee, flying along from the side door. His confessional canonicals and arm stole were flapping wildly in the wind.

Only one thought occurred to me. My last minute parliamentary selection had been in all the papers, and he must be delighted in my progress The great wee man was determined, the unwritten protocols of the anonymous sacrament to one side, to take this one opportunity to congratulate me. Hastily, and painfully, I snigged my brand new fag 'tween finger and thumb, grimacing away the pain. As he drew alongside, that thought quickly vanished, his face was ashen: "I'm very very, disappointed in you Paddy, very disappointed indeed; you have just made a *Bad Confession*, so you have".

Two things still remembered; my lower lip trembled in shock. My airless throat so dry I thought I was choking. The gang of unemployed men at their Saturday morning meeting place for a fag and a chinwag in the crescent gateway, had heard the charge. They turned as one, gaping through the rails, fags suspended in their knuckles. There were men there of near retirement age who had never found work. Nor had they ever heard anything like this.

A *bad confession*. What had the Christian Brothers along this very road told me?

A reserved sin to be cleansed only by a bishop. Or was it that one "better that a millstone be tied round my neck and hurled into the depths of the ocean,"—was it that bit of the terror threats of final damnation in my penny catechism ? I had total recall of the prayer-book picture of a silver-booted St. Michael the Archangel with his huge silver sword ramming Satan down and down to the gates of hell. Was I now under him too, doomed? What chance Paddy McGarvey, Labour Candidate, Mid-Ulster, here read out at the church door, getting to Westminster while avoiding Hell?

I stammered my first question, and tried to smile. What on this earth did he mean? Earth was the wrong place. This was Heaven's charge. The priest was bursting with holy venom.

"Socialists." he raged. "You are consorting with socialists now and you did not confess it. Socialism is a serious occasion of sin and you should have nothing to do with it. You have joined the Labour Party, and by betraying the church, you are denying Christ."

I tried to tell this grand wee priest that just across the water in Lancashire, the Catholic Church in constant supplication for state aid to our schools was heavily reliant on the Labour party. Many of Lancashire's MPs at that time were Catholics. Then I had a stronger straw to grasp, or so I thought.

"Listen Father, you're confusing us with Godless communism. The Labour Party originates in the social teaching of the Methodist Church, and listen now, look here Father, the chairman of the party is England's best known Catholic, a convert actually, the Earl of Longford."

"Lord Longford's soul is a matter for his own concern. It has nothing to do with your's". He strode away, back to the Confession Box, still in a right strop. Then, and moreso now, revising this in the autumn of my life, I had always thought of Christ, a good socialist, whipping the money-lending bankers out of the Temple. It is happening still.

No British Mass-going Catholic in full communion would ever think for a moment he was in a state of sin as a Labour card holder, but to be fair to my great wee priest, he had a point about the party's leader. The 7th Earl of a settled Cromwellian family in Ireland, the Pakenhams, was in flux between his job and the church. Lord Longford's great friend and patron in the party, its leader Hugh Gaitskell, had died suddenly of a mysterious infection the year before, 1963. The friendship had survived their rivalry in both proposing to the beauteous Elizabeth Harman, a real life Zulieka Dobson of their days at girl-rare Oxford in the 'twenties. Frank Pakenham won the girl, who said she had never seen so ugly a man when found lying asleep, mouth hanging open, hair askew, all four limbs spreadeagled on a May Ball sofa A biography, Lord Longford, published thirty years later by Hieneman in 1994, has this by the author, Peter Stanford, a former editor of the Catholic Herald. (*With permission here, agents A.P. Watt*).

"Longford's daughter Antonia, herself by now on demand as a Catholic commentator on radio and television, but taking a softer line than her father on moral matters, recalls an argument over Conservative plans, backed wholeheartedly by Labour, to make contraceptive pills freely available on the National Health Service.

'He stuck at nothing in condemnation of that. When I tried to talk about the real world, he wouldn't have any of it I think anytime in politics where the doctrine of the Catholic Church pointed one way and the doctrine of the Labour Party another, he stuck with the Church.'

A man for Father McKee every time, but he stayed in the party. Every party in a democracy has to be a coalition of itself. Labour would scrape into continued power, seeking reinforcement in '66. Gaitskell's successor, Harold Wilson, was persuaded by Cabinet survivors from the great reforming Attlee Government of 1945-51 to make Longford his Leader in the Lords. His Tory opponent, the holder of a unique Irish peerage still seated there, Lord Carrington, applauded his brilliant sense of balance—"an innovator, yet accepted as one of us". Sainthood-type services in Britain would come later, not least for me his ready patronage of the charity-based research engine I would establish to scrutinise the needling Anglo-Irish wish for a solution.

As I walked out the church gate, driven out, the representatives of Northern Ireland's seven per cent unemployed, 39 per cent in some individual towns, some my own age who had never been employed, they all avoided my eye. What they had seen and heard was as much a shock to them, and it would be all over the town that evening.

For a moment I had tapped and opened the nerve centre at the politics of many priests at the time, an underlay of corrosive Catholic Fascism, enriched Irish fruit from the Spanish Civil War, and undisturbed by what ethnic horrors had happened before and during the second World War. That evening Jimmy drove me to the airport in an hour of silence to return to a country he regarded as "pagan".

Well, they were all wrong. Somebody Up There must have been watching. Well before the twenty-fourth hour since my damnation in Armagh, I was standing in the sacristy of one of the most Catholic churches in Christendom, about to serve holy Mass in Brompton Oratory. British European Airways were still disembarking Heathrow passengers by bus in

Kensington High Street. I persuaded the driver to let me off in Brompton Road; yards from the church, and barely into it, I was grabbed by a flunkey in green knee breeches and off-white stockings asking me if I could serve Mass. Too surprised to warn him I had been sort of "read out" and anyway not cognisant with the "New Mass" I numbly assented.

"Listen" he warned, "the priest's German and he's very old; you will have to help him as well."

Help a priest to say Mass! I took this as a divine Post-It Note from a passing angel that I was well and truly back in the ranks, no longer church-martialled, a soldier once again of the Church Militant, even as that version faded from view for so many about to leave by the million. In the Vestry I felt at home again, waiting for Father Fritz to robe up, encouraged by a wee fat gilded cherub on the wall brandishing a lyre at me. Brompton Oratory is grossly baroque to Anglo Irish eyes. Well at least it wasn't a bow and arrow he was aiming, or St. Michael the Archangel doing an Errol Flynn on me with his bloody great sword. As for his Mass, if it was to be in the German vernacular, I could pretend it was Latin, which wouldn't "feel" as inadequate as the new one. By "feel" here I mean grace. Until then it was common, even for grown worldly men, to obtain grace at Mass, especially when still in the wash of a "good confession". The Mass reformers, trying a Vox Pop of the Faithful, were nonplussed by one old lady's brusque response: "it interferes with me prayers."

Pope Paul's new Mass was conceived in the lunacy of change for its own sake, the early versions encumbered with a catch-all liturgy of leaping, jumping, kneeling and standing, embracing your neighbours and dancing in the aisles, while at Pentecost chucking money into giant tubs. Some or all of this was signalled by the finger-flicking priest facing us from the wooden tables interposed to the marble altar, as he waffled through interminable non-stop banalities as "wine, the work of human hands". It could hardly be the work of clock hands, the chosen limb wrong as well. Every Mass-going omadaun (Irish=idiot) like me in remotest rural Ireland, regions not noticeable for vineyards or consumption of the produce thereof, knows full well wine is the work of human feet, hardly pigs's feet either, a popular dish in those same parts. "Religious gym" my own parish priest in Bury St. Edmunds dubbed it. Bryan Houghton, the rebel convert priest who resigned his ministry in 1969, but not his priesthood, called for a new order of clergy to deal with it OHM, the Order of the Holy Microphone.

I had the unhappy duty, he asked of me, to organise a press conference for his resignation. Every London daily newspaper attended it. I had duties elsewhere for my Sunday paper. Days before, sharing a drink with me in the Presbytery, he defended the traditional Mass.

"There are four people attending it, McGarvey. There is the scholar reading the Missal in Latin, the teacher following it in the English translation alongside. Then there is the partly educated reading the beautiful books which follow the Ordinary of the Mass, like St. Anthony's Bread or the Treasury of the Sacred Heart, and finally McGarvey, if you don't mind me saying so, there's the Irish washerwoman clacking her beads. You need not be offended when I tell you which of them is the most devout, the most attentive. You have only one guess".

Brompton Oratory's shallow sanctuary had no room for the temporary table between the steps of the high altar and the communion rail. Priests all over, where this situation was common, were struggling with the new Mass on the old altars, their backs to the congregation as for centuries yore. I gripped the feeble old man by his forearm to help him up the steps. He was so surprised he fell over on all fours, wrenching his arm away and I thought he had fainted. Pulling himself up with the aid of the steps and then kneeling on the first one, was a clue to what was about to happen.

"*Introibo ad altare Dei*"* he said pointedly at me, and Master Louis Doyle's Latin scholar from Greenpark CBS Grammar School, Armagh, who could read Caesar's Gallic Wars backwards, was flying. I gave him the works, the words, the wine, the water, while gently tapping the welkin of four wee bells to softly alert the faithful to the arrival of Christ in the Sacrament. I felt myself earning grace that washed away my public disgrace of the day before—not that I rejoiced or justified myself in hurting that grand wee priest. Goodness me, in the wave of absolution now annointing me, I felt maybe I could even win Mid Ulster for Labour! More seriously, this was a measure of grace I believe the Catholic Church can no longer deliver at Pope Paul's verbose and stony Mass

*I will go unto the altar of God.

Duncan "Tommy" Webb, the journalist on The People who broke up the brothel and street prostitution rings of the Malta gangs in central London during the 'Fifties, had to spend his working days visiting such places, frequently as a pretending, checking customer before uttering, after establishing a tart's verbal contract, the deathless phrase by which he is remembered still: *"I made an excuse and left"*.

He died young, barely turned 40 in 1958. I was on the News Chronicle, The People's Associate Editor Charles "Laurie" Manifold, a family visitor to mine, asked me to arrange a memorial service for him in a Catholic Church, official approaches having failed, perhaps because The People, as well as being the independent Sunday sister to the official organ of the Labour party, the Daily Herald, was also published by Odham's Press, Jewish owned. And so I did, eventually kneeling in St. Cecilia's, Southampton Row, behind three rows of Jewish executives most of them wearing yarmulkas. (Why can't we have a new religion as Judeo-Christians!) The church was only a short walk from the Odhams newsrooms in Endell Street. I did it all again at the same church for Gilbert Harding, the great panjandrum of British TV, and a People columnist, only weeks after I interviewed him. Dying from lung cancer, he was still smoking. because, he told me: on the phone from his home, "I am really a very weak-willed man". Millions of his TV fans, or the readers of his thunderous prose, would never believe it.

Beside me in St. Cecilia's was the staff photographer who most frequently accompanied Webb. Stan Jaanus, the son of a Lithuanian seaman, grew up in the docklands of Bermondsey, on the south bank of the Thames, and looked it, more docker than photographer, the other reason why he was chosen. I murmured something about all this ceremonial being a big change for poor old Tommy. Stan rebuffed me, all surprised, he said, at hearing this from another Catholic. He had, nearly all times, picked him up after early morning Mass from a Catholic church.

Webb told him he could not possibly do this dangerous, seedy work without seeking the grace and strength he could get at daily Mass. Paradoxically, and not taking the Mick, I remember thinking in the silence of taking this in, lots of tarts in my own experience, go to daily Mass too. The Mass that Duncan "Tommy" Webb needed daily, had the accrued wisdom and solace honed by centuries, and the apprentice carpenter from Nazareth. As I keep saying, it did not need fixing.

* * *

AFTER GINA, RITA AND GRETA, JACK'S RITA (With Tea and Love-Hearts)

Talk of the Malta gangs in London and recalling Charles "Laurie" Manifold in that last tale reminds me of the time he sent me round to Edgeware Road to interview Soho's criminal mastermind, Jack Spot. As well as being singled out by The Guardian as the greatest ever organiser and director of in-depth reporting, the first of many accolades from other newspapers, The People's associate editor was a distinctive racing driver, but restricted himself to the newish version called Motocross. They raced standard saloon cars, in his case the VW Beetle, over mixed circuits of ploughed land and meadow. Great fun.

Jack wasn't in and I was welcomed at his door by his wife, Rita Comer. She invited me in, explaining Comer would be back soon, just out and around doing some shopping. Two things you must know about Rita; she would give Rita Hayworth a double pass for looks, a Windmill show girl when Spot met her, and she had the most delicious Dublin accent you ever heard outside The Coombe. Over tea and love-hearts (minute iced biscuits) we recalled our days in dear old dirty Dublin, remembering Johnny Forty Coats, or the Double-Decker Sheriff shooting pedestrians from the bus platform, and other well loved tramps, until the reverie was ended by noises at the door and in strode Mr. Menace himself.

Comer was a huge man, and his long black Ulster topcoat right down to his ankles added more of the same, the height this time emphasised by two bulging bags of provender of all kinds hanging from each hand. Seeing any man with shopping bags then was unusual, but then so was Jack Spot. Both were dropped without ceremony so that, as I stood up out of courtesy, he could grip me by the lapels of my raincoat, my jacket and my shirt, all clamped together in his huge hands, to lift me clean off the floor. I weighed nearly 14 stone.

He held me there as Rita cried I was just a nice Irish boy she was talking to. Jesus, Mary and Joseph, Jack, will you put the poor boy down, she sang out in her Dublin patois.

Cromer "Who're you boy?" and I managed to croak my name.

Cromer "And who sent ya'?"

Me "The People, Laurie Manifold."

I was dropped as suddenly as the "shopping" bags, otherwise known in Soho's restaurants and delis as Jack Spot's rent

Cromer "Wot, 'im? Webbie's getaway driver."

When I indicated an interview he indicated the door. Some days you learn more out of the office than in. Rita gave me an unopened bag of her love-hearts. I can't remember what Laurie said when I asked him if he had been "Webbie's getaway driver?" But I'm sure he didn't start from Holy Mass.

CHAPTER TEN

Campaigning in Ulster

After my Teutonic Latin Mass at Brompton—"*my Mass!*"—we are still in 1964, a friend drove my toilet-paper toned Triumph Vitesse in from Suffolk, to take to Ireland, the only way Lloyds would insure my election-driving. It's in the United Kingdom, I argued with an insurance broker in Poultry EC1. It's still in Ireland he countered. They would only insure my own personal car. Super-Pam (neighbours' and friends' accolade) came too with more over and under pants, my typewriter and other word weaponry, I had to stay in London, to square my news desk which meant calming my news editor on the Sunday Mirror, Cliff Pearson, who had raised a row about my sudden delve into politics. Although living by choice out in the civilised remoteness of Bury St. Edmunds, seventy miles from the office, and where our children could walk to schools just yards from the doorstep of a £2000 five-bedroom Regency townhouse, I was frequently summoned back from my Eastern region to handle heavy stuff for London.

The tall, lumbering Cliff was the greatest all-out supporting news editor, no matter whatever or wherever the story, I ever experienced, and notoriously miserable with expenses on taxis, buses or trains but Croesus-like himself when aroused by a big story. He once chartered a DeHavilland Rapide light airliner for me to bring a tug-of-love baby girl back to England from Dublin, so that we would not be bothered by rivals. It didn't work. Awaiting a decision of the court on the airport apron, a nurse called Charmian flew in from Wales to join me, causing the flap she was the wife of Ronnie Biggs, the escaped train robber, joining her husband, me.

The Court said no, and I sang the Bard of Armagh to convince a squad of Gardai armed with short-barrel machine guns that I too was from Armagh.

Cliff was rebuffed by a Mirror rule of thumb that staff could be loaned to the Labour Party at elections, whether candidates or publicists. Its left-wing origins are obscure, less evident when it was founded as a woman's paper by Northcliffe himself. In my times it was owned by a member of the Ellerman Lines shipping family, a remote figure living permanently in The Dorchester Hotel. In parliament, when Labour MPs ragged the Tory-supporting press, the Tories shouted back: "Who owns the Daily Mirror?" The answer was—the Sunday Mirror, or the other way round. No one quite knew.

Thus forearmed, and Mid-Ulster forewarned, I sallied home—my original homeland that is—for the first time to do battle for my beleaguered people, a Labour NEC candidate on loan to the Northern Ireland Labour Party, which meant I was now a unionist with a small "u". This wayward son of a star orator on Hibernian platforms, a Nationalist Armagh council chairman for many first years of the century, a stage raconteur and singer for church charities, the confidante and press adviser to three cardinals, was now a traitor, a turncoat. Taking the British shilling, the Queen's McGarvey, as regarded by some editorial grumblers in Dublin papers, I was stoutly defended in the national language by the Irish Independent columnist Prionsais MacAonghusa To my shame I have never read a translation.

My sudden selection for Mid Ulster had naturally alarmed my brother Jimmy, whose mission in life, alongside his exceptional work and book-value performance for the mighty Prudential—their No I Star Operator for several years—was to continue my father's press work for the Cardinal Primates (One of my abstemious brother's rewards from the Pru was an abstemious post-war lunch in London with Britain's most frugal Chancellor, "Work or Want" Sir Stafford Cripps. Almost certainly, his main course was snoek, (whale-meat pretending to be a steak) The very last Cardinal he served was Tomais O'Fiach, (and betimes a new friend, Church of Ireland Primate, Archbishop Otto Simms) who as priesthood student Tommy Fee had shared tuition of (mostly) girls's Irish language classes with him, and an Armagh teacher on the Lough Neagh shore at Collegeland. Young seminarian Fee fell in love on that shore and left Maynooth, Ireland's lead seminary to the priesthood, now a university college with women students. The lakeside romance did not gell for him, a situation eventually opening his return to the church that would take him to its Irish peak (with wider experience than most seminarians). That absence was explained in his obituaries as failing health. Wouldn't you think the Church would prefer to make the point that for a robust young fellow from South Armagh, celibacy is a daunting challenge. Armagh joked that the church was run by the pair of them, Tommy Fee and our Jimmy, in Irish, in the kitchen. During a previous reign the city council's yard foreman, Benny Hamilton, shouted at the ace reporter home from Fleet Street, across the Shambles Corner: "Cardinals come and cardinals go, but your fella takes them out in the yard and marks them" a ribald allusion to the procedure in the local pig market. Cardinal O'Fiach was a more open Republican than County Tyrone's fierce Joe MacRory, a crag-faced Mount Rushmore figure resolutely opposed to military conscription for the North in January 1942 from the envoys of Roosevelt and Churchill (my father in the kitchen?). What else could Tom Fee be, born in Cullyhanna, the middle of Bandit Country by the time he came home to get Rome's red hat? When Jimmy lay dying on August 29th 1981, by his choice in Armagh County Infirmary for the ease of his young family—he was only 58, stricken by a glandular form of TB,—the Cardinal Prince of the Irish church sat at his bedside, all day, my brother's last day. So it was understandable that back there in 1964 Jimmy had motored over to Omagh to have it out with me. He had dabbled in politics himself as a city Nationalist councillor with the biggest personal vote ever recorded, but found it not to his liking and resigned. I sent him home with the reassurance that I could not possibly win this one, not yet. I did not stand again in 1966. Our children, our beloved, and my great friends (for most of the time), but nevertheless "the enemies of promise" (Cyril Connolly's, the pram in the hallway) to politicians as much as to freelance hack writers, were coming to serious exams and school changes. In the interval a ranting, self-annointed churchless Protestant cleric, guess who, marched up the Falls Road with a straggle of followers to break the window of a bicycle shop and wrench from inside a display of tiny, two-inch enamel flags of nations, for choice to clip on your front mudguard. The traitorous owner of the shop, so obviously "An Enemy of Ulster", had included the Irish tricolour. The dawn of sanity I had visualised for this endeavour, and for which I had turned down invitations to two marginal seats in Britain, South Cambridge, and winnable Eton and Slough, was proved false. Northern Ireland, whatever it was before, was never to be as peaceful again.

* * *

1963 INTERLUDE *APRES* LUNCH WITH A PRIME MINISTER

Monty Court was a brilliant sports writer who transmogrified himself into News Editor of The Daily Mail, an amazing career leap across the tramlines of British journalism, whereupon he had a big problem one day in June 1963 and so naturally, he called on me.

'Look Paddy" he declared down seventy miles of antique telephone lines to remote Bury St. Edmunds, 'three Labour prime ministers have just been elected in the Caribbean and all three are coming to the Test on Saturday'—*

(June 6-10th West Indies winning the Wisden Trophy by ten wickets at Old Trafford.)

'We want you to nip over to Cambridge, where Supermac is lunching with Professor Trevor-Roper at Peterhouse and ask him if he will host the three West Indian premiers at the cricket. Good idea, eh Paddy? Mum's the word, and I'm relying on you, OK! Our exclusive, understood?'

To say I "swallowed hard" would be an understatement. In those years you didn't, because you couldn't, buttonhole the Prime Minister just like that, and certainly not one so serenly remote as Harold Macmillan. Even for a news-editor who also knew his geography—unlike Monty few of mine ever did—I saw little chance of getting into a master's lodge, at lunchtime uninvited, at any Cambridge college. They too often savour the hope that a big idea can be kept exclusive even when a Prime Minister is in the story, something Downing Street would never permit. Just think of the rage of the rivals. Monty chose me, thirty miles away, for fear the busy Cambridge News Agency would plunder his idea for all their other customers, even though. I had no working connection with the Mail at the time. As I was drawing breath, he sensed my hesitation: 'Paddy, win or lose, fifty quid' about four months mortgage instalments. I ran to the Catholic Church just down the street where my car was parked in the school yard next door, a parish indulgence. After a cautious Hail Mary for the adventurous day without accident (well it was for the Daily Mail). I arrived at Peterhouse Master's Lodge just as the door was opening. McGarvey *dead on* again.

My immediate problem was the half-circle of Cambridge City Constabulary in braided 19th century dress-uniforms under shako-style helmets, shoulder to shoulder around the steps. They were all facing the door. Not a single truncheon could be wedged between them. *Tight security, still,* was a cliche newly born, but not here, so nothing for it but a gentle push from behind, uttering 'Excuse me please' in my brash Ulster accent. Amazing even for then, they let me through, shuffling sideways on silent shoes with murmured apologies.

Pause, while you think of an Ulsterman trying that six years later.

Harold Macmillan had his back to me, saying his farewells. I introduced myself as he turned, a squadron of butterflies churning my stomach. I was also discombobulated by his height, me a standard 5'9", him a former Guards officer (Grenadiers) and one final curved step above me. : "Good afternoon Prime Minister, I'm from The Daily Mail."

'Good gracious' he exclaimed, both hands up. He swayed back on his heels in mock feint at such effrontery, declaring 'The Daily Mail is a bloody awful newspaper.' I laughed. He laughed. Professor Hugh Trevor Roper, lurking just behind him, led the others, all laughing heartily. Some of it was "*Prime Minister made-a-joke-so-everybody—laugh*, but Supermac—the nickname was bestowed, and it stuck, by the cartoonist Vicky—was echoing an old saw by the Duke of Edinburgh years before, one of his first public utterances 'The *Daily Express* is a bloody awful newspaper'.

Joke over, he affected a calmer mode with tilted head in questing fashion. This was his favourite pose, Downing Street's greatest thespian since Disraeli, acting now as the grave Father of the Nation—as Douglas Hurd, a former aide, often recalled. Alastair Horne, his earlier official biographer * would speak of his "*charm and mischief*" and "*an ever-wily politician in his use of flippancy to conceal himself.*" I was getting all of that, with both barrels. Some of it also concealed real painful discomforts from three successive wounds in the Flanders trenches. A deeper family hurt for concealment came from the infidelity of his ducal Devonshire wife with another MP, but endured as the marriage held.

* *Volume One—Macmillan 1891-1956—(Macmillan 1988)*

'Well now, how can we help the Daily Mail?' and I put Monty's question.'
'Well, you know, the Daily Mail is also a silly paper. Surely they must know it's the Trooping of the Colour on Saturday and that I'm a former Guardsman. I shall be trooping the colour with Her Majesty—never the Test. I don't go to the Tests dear boy'

Trooping the Colour that Saturday, June 8th, were the Coldstream Guards, 2nd Battalion. His rejection and explanation nevertheless made decent copy, and I had made money, successfully. Pleased with myself, a big notch on my belt, it had gone so well, I thanked him with all the grace my Edwardian father had taught me (the behaviour was catching), and turned down the steps. Even the cops were chortling. Back in the station they would slap their thighs and rechortle it all again 'What a card, eh? Then came the summons.

"I say, I say look here, look here" and I turned to find the Prime Minister beckoning me back up again. (clearly getting into his stride now, a politician on a platform, with listeners all around, behind and below).

The jacket of his silver-grey Prince-of-Wales-check suit was flipped open. He looked just like a typical patrician tipping a porter, and for a moment I thought that's what he was going to do, with me. He dived into a waistcoat pocket and extracted a huge gold coin and waved it under my nose. I was now near enough to see it was not a coin, it was a medal.

'I'm an old railwayman as well, you know—would you like to see my Director's Medal? Great Western of course, but it takes me everywhere, God's Wonderful Railway indeed'. Everybody now gathered round exclaiming Ohs and Ahs:

'I don't suppose the Daily Mail knew that either'

Finally, the former political manager of the 8th army campaign in the desert and Italy let me go. The cops were breaking up.

I wrote it deadpan, word for word, exactly as it happened, none of which appeared in The Daily Mail, or anywhere else until now. I kept my word to Monty, who paid my fifty quid.

Forty-five years on, writing that for here, I needed dates, but Peterhouse College found they had no record of the Prime Minister lunching in Master's Lodge. Helpful to my research, an archivist concluded that it must have been "a non university event."

A month later, thanks to added research guidance from the college's Ward Library, and then Google, I stumbled on Macmillan's shattering announcement in the Commons on July 10 1963, only four weeks after the Peterhouse lunch, that Kim Philby, who had just fled from his Observer newspaper berth in Beirut aboard a rapidly turned-round Soviet freighter, was indeed a traitor and spy, the former recruiter and leader of the "Cambridge Five".

Hugh Trevor Roper, not Master of Peterhouse until a few years later, was an intelligence consultant, an author on espionage. Supermac's Cambridge lunch was a last-ditch conference with his counter-espionage experts, at the scene of the crimes you could say—to do or deny on admissions, but finally to pin down Philby's guilt.

My arrival on that doorstep after that lunch must have given 'unflappable' Supermac more than a mild fright. How well he concealed it.

But the man from the Daily Mail only wanted to talk about the cricket and three new Labour prime ministers from the Caribbean—As Private Eye might have put it then—Large doubles all round!

CHAPTER ELEVEN

1964 More Mid Ulster

Phelim O'Neill, with a name like that, an obvious scion of Irish royalty, had the O'Neill flair for making something out of nothing; one easy example, me, as a last-minute candidate parachuted into the second largest constituency in the United Kingdom. The election declared, Phelim, general secretary of a textile trade union (for women only) wrote to the Belfast office of the Northern Ireland Labour Party complaining Mid Ulster, alone of the province's eleven Westminster seats, didn't have a candidate. By return of post he got me. Like me also married in England to a nice English girl who insisted on presenting him with a schoolroom of children, one more than our seven, he was trying to establish themselves in his home town of Omagh. Work was scarce. The nearby town of Strabane was frequently producing horrific unemployment percentages on the BBC monthly bulletins, 39 per cent for male workers when the Ulster average was a "scandalous" six or seven, Britain's was 2.5%, which in practical terms meant full employment. To stop employers hoarding labour in Britain, an almost surreal situation, the Tories had imposed a head tax on them, SET—Selective Employment Tax.

Throughout the North there was a substantial payroll of low paid females in the clothing factories. In macho male trade unions their conditions were virtually ignored. Social and religious sectarianism was really three-way. To Protestants and Catholics, just add women. Phelim's answer was to form a separate trade union for them. Such gender selection is probably illegal now, but the union flourished in spite of factory closures and fluctuating contracts for the big British brands and chain stores. The boyish male with the sandy skin under a thin red beard, still in his thirties, was accepted by the giggling younger bench workers only when their elders, the working

Mamas and Grannies decided he needed looking after himself. They adopted him, while he organised them.

My selection was a walkover because the vibrant Omagh branch of the Union of Post Office Workers, bursting to have a go to help rid the country, the entire United Kingdom that is, of a union-hostile Postmaster General, Reginald Bevins. They had failed to produce one of their own, all of them employees who could not afford the risk of relinquishing their jobs. Why they had not picked Phelim had something to do with the Irish social view that a member of parliament had to be educated to grammar school level at least, from above the common working stock, and devoid of flamboyant character or weird associations. Unlike the reverse in Britain, even after Blair and his university socialists ruined the party, a Labour government's deputy prime minister was a former ship's steward, and a postman, Alan Johnston, was the Minister for Education, Home Secretary, and in opposition, Shadow Chancellor; yet as my campaign swung into action I already had a clear impression that Phelim had the better CV, in experience and attitudes, for parliament. I have long since concluded as a watcher on the ditch, that journalists in particular make lousy politicians. I did ask why he wasn't chosen and was told "Phelim the candidate! You must be joking. He runs a trade union for wimmin. fer God's sake—no chance."—Macho Ulster, its other prejudice. With me as his Sancho Panza the brilliant Phelim, as a natural outsider, might prove them wrong. Come to think of it, we were both outsiders

First things first, said Phelim, only minutes after my selection. "I'm going to show you your constituency," guiding my car to the outskirts of Omagh, and surprisingly soon, up a narrow winding mountain road. The Gortin Gap is an abutment of The Sperrins, a long range of stony hill farms and moorland bird havens. The evening sky was darkening and I thought this was foolhardy. I had not reckoned with the gloaming, holding the mid-September daylight in a long, slow fadeout to a final curtain, which way up here even in September can be close to midnight. At the top Phelim was out of the car and scrambling up a four-foot embankment. With a circumference sweep of his arms he exclaimed: "There you are Paddy, Mid-Ulster at your feet." Not actually fat, but comfortably overweight at fourteen stone, I had some difficulty in clambering up alongside him to see what was on offer. Suppressing a laugh, the Temptation of Christ on the Mountain top slipped in and out of my thinking.

From up here, looking down, this part of the Emerald Isle looked boggy brown, relieved by the silvery flashes of small ice-age lakes. Away to the west a red white and blue sky hung over a much longer silver streak, the Atlantic's own horizon. To the east, the populous east, nothing, no town, just more brown, not even a farm.

"My God, Phelim, I can't see a single bloody voter anywhere."

"You needn't fret, you don't have to see them yet. You'll meet them all in their infinite variety and sobriety". My election agent is a prose poet; it was going to be an Irish election here. The first Mid-Ulster voters I met were in their underwear, that is, Phelim's female membrship in their underwear.

They were deeply respectable members of Phelim's union of women, standing in as models at the Cookstown bra and girdle factory he insisted we tour. Daintyfyt, The managers were mostly career firemen from a parent British textile group. They acceded readily to a poll-time tour by an election candidate as something normal in the English hustings, but quite off the wall here. So there I was beaming at benches of giggling girls, many of them too young to vote anyway, wondering what Father McKee would have said about this.

"This is an occasion of sin—I warned you Paddy" surely. More of an occasion of embarrassment. I thought we were getting away with the random wall posters of the company's product advertising, which in those innocent years—the 'Sixties hysteria was a latecomer to Ulster—were devoid of all sexual lubricity, but lo, the English enthusiasts had called on some comely Tyrone matrons to stand at tactical points of the tour wearing the company tops and bottoms between plump spaces of pale goosebumps. One shy smiler even gave me a little curtsy, as if genuflecting to a bishop. My other hand safely ensconced in my jacket pocket, my head stooped forward, the very model of a suitably po-faced MP, for the first and last time in my life I gravely shook hands with a lady in her bra and girdle.

Our next encounter with the voters of Mid-Ulster had to be very different, but again, mainly female. Phelim's political instincts now led us to the substantial Co. Derry village of Swatragh, where a typical crumbling rural economy had been transformed by a brilliant socialist curate of the kind Ireland lacks in spades. The remarkable Father Seamus Shields died tragically young in a car crash, but not before he had successfully guided the Swatraghans to transform themselves into a vibrant rural co-operative society, roping in everything from horticulture to home baking. Although it did not seem to match the awakening giants of dairy husbandry in the South, it was a model to others in the North. Phelim's theory was simple: "A co-operative village is bound to vote Labour." Ever the optimist, Phelim.

We parked my Triumph Vitesse and the Tannoy loudspeaker van close to the centre and prepared to launch the workers's clarion call. The first reaction was exciting, a solid regime of over a hundred women began forming on the pavements a little way up the hill—an actual audience!! They remained there until Phelim opened proceedings, whereupon they started marching towards us, an unbroken line of female river-trance, and yet reducing in numbers. Pre-arranged groups were vanishing up the entries, the gated 19th century archways to the stabling and yards at the rear. Next came a peal of thunder that rose in such a crescendo it felt like a squadron of bombers overhead. Phelim had to give up attempts at speech with despairing out-flung arms. It now seemed to be coming over the rooftops. I ran up to one of the alleys and was amazed to see women and girls kneeling or hunkering down to bang bin lids on the rough stony ground, shiny bright new bin lids. They must have been placed there beforehand. Swatragh Co-Operative's hardware division must have cornered the market on steel bins, finding a novel use for them in election year—the one election year everybody knew had to come. Using refuse bins to refuse Labour a voice was funny were it not so serious, an irony of history you could say. The decibel level was well above human endurance, frightening for anyone living close by and unaware of the origin. I signalled with waving down-turned palms to my three supporters to pack it in and pack up. At that a wide cordon of men now appeared across the top of the street, nearly all carrying new zinc buckets this time. This scene, the women, then the men, in advancing lines, echoed in my mind the moment I saw Riverdance thirty years later. They began hurling small white missiles that looked like bread rolls and I remember my natural socialism boiling up at their unthinking indulgence with the staff of life; even if it was stale it felt sinful. We quietly ignored the fusilades of stuff dropping over us while dismantling our equipment, turned away and left Swatragh to the future war that would surround it while sparing it. Back over the high moonlit Sperrins we made our way to Omagh, which would not be spared. Less than a decade on from that election, Swatragh's bin-lid tocsins would become a universal Catholic answer to the ceremonial Lambeg drums whipping up Protestant ire. Rattling bin lids along streets warned of the presence of Government forces. My anger turned to a measure of mirth as we drew away; the women of Swatragh had seen off the enemy, no mistake, and not a word exchanged or a brick thrown.

There was some comfort in the beauty of that late September night, driving across the roof of this beautiful, tragic constituency and slowing down to gaze across the glittering roadside lakes. The whitening grassy shores signalled a hard early frost. No romantic Hollywood studio could have conjured such an ethereal combination of land, lake, the moon and the starry sky—a rural Mid-Ulster indeed.

In the morning, after a typical hard Irish night on tea and stout, dressing in the front bedroom of a postman's house where I was harboured and fed, I was curious as to who had arrived so early in the bright yellow car parked in front, directly under my window. My query at the breakfast table brought everyone to the front door, and of course, the car was mine. I was mistaken about the unsocialist Swatraghhans abusing bread. They had been throwing eggs, rotten and lots of them from those buckets, to which recipe the high Sperrins had added a slender skein of ice. My Triumph Vitesse, from the factory an off-white shade of the cheapest government office toilet paper, was transformed, enhanced even, as *Vitesse Oeuf Frappe*. We all had a good laugh. The pain came later, in the hours it took to carefully scrape it all off. I wondered what the insurance executive in Poultry E1 would think of those eggs.

It was men only in the confrontation that followed in the gauntly beautiful village of Stewartstown, as planter a name as any you'll get in Scottish Ulster. High three story 18th century houses, unusual in that size and period to be terraced together in a village, are in ranks around a sizable square. Rare English villages of similar build and period, described as "hall houses," were said to have been made "for the carriage trade," so that the newly rich trading classes could the more easily co-host each other with events, dinners and balls, just as their bettors did in the great houses. Near our home in Bury St. Edmunds there was a short street of them at the centre. This one was a primly tidy village, the square then resembled nothing so much as a faded backdrop to a Disney fairy tale with Gothic overtones. Here Phelim's purpose was to beard the lion in his den, and indeed, something of a Disney episode resulted. The lion rose to the bait, bared his teeth—only inches away from mine—but did not bite.

We set up our sound system directed at the particular exit street which contained the premises of an auctioneer, a publican, and an MP, all three in the persona of one Mr. George Forrest, the Mid-Ulster incumbent for eight years since he won the seat fair and fairly square after disputes involving the High Court and Parliament itself in 1956. Its tangled history began the year before when it was won in the Westminster general election of May 1955 by a convicted IRA bomber in prison, Tom Mitchell, standing as abstentionist Sinn Fein, with 29,737 votes. It was declared void because he was a convicted felon. The by-election that following October was won again by Mitchell, defeating the same Unionist candidate, Mr. Charles Beattie. Mitchell constitutionally barred again, the High Court declared Beattie the winner. It then transpired that he too was statute-barred as holding "an office of profit under the Crown"—two in fact. He was a paid member of tribunals for National Insurance and National Assistance cases. At the next attempt, Mitchell standing yet again, he was defeated by Forrest standing as an independent Unionist, whereupon he joined the party. The indefatigable Mitchell, the bomber turned Dublin Corporation housing inspector if you please, stood in 1955 (twice), 1956, 1959, 1964 against me and Forrest, and finally in 1966, a steadfast man, quiet and courteous, it had to be said by his opponents. Six years later when I organised a meeting of North-South parliamentarians (I was the first to do so) at St. Michael's College, Omeath, he turned up with his agent to listen, but did not speak.

So here we are on Mr. Forrest's front doorstep. Someone made a quick sally from the pub to check it was us making the noise, dived back in again, whereupon a single file of silent men emerged, clearly pre-arranged, displaying marching experience—Orangemen and B-Men, no doubt, some of them both.

Fortified inwardly with a dark brew made by Dublin Protestants, they would now defend Ulster from Popery, Brass Money and Wooden Shoes, but hang on a minute, this Fenian was not one of them fenians, and not against the Union, so what was he? Answer, they formed ranks in front of us, standing still and silent only eighteen inches from our soapbox, hands to their sides. I continued my speech with a noticeable tremor, and then the boss himself came out. There can rarely have been an election husting anywhere in these islands for at least a century where a candidate has the sitting member in his audience. George Forrest leaned on his street corner listening to me, and chatting with four RUC men who suddenly appeared alongside him. Another pre-arranged signal unknown to us brought him out into the Square.

His men, his customers, they were paying him, parted lines to let him through, and close enough to raise a clenched fist between his chin and mine. Shaking it he complained: "Listen Mister, I AM George Forrest the MP and you're telling lies about me, so you are."

My Sunday Express election address had clearly sunk home. What struck me was his wounded air of a poor put-upon country boy, the more surprising against his appearance, a dapper handsome man in a suit that was not tailored in Ireland. Always well turned out, he looked more like the traditional Land Agent, far from the rumpled scruffy appearance of most MPs. Out of the corner of my eye I could see the RUC boys rolling about, slapping their upraised thighs in gales of laughter—"Man dear, thon George is the Quare Boy right enough"

My Edwardian manners, honed by my widower father, who had me taught at seven how to open and eat Carlingford oysters in Warrenpoint, and never go anywhere new with your two hands the one length, bearing a gift he meant, bid that I should respond, politely, but that would have broken the meeting, ending what we wanted to say. What we were saying, and where we were saying it, was novel to Northern Ireland's backroom, indoor hustings in hired one-party halls. It was allied to the proper candidate selection process Labour was using in Ireland, in contrast to the usual Irish "rump" system based on who knows who. Outside Belfast we rarely had any trouble in the streets. To be candid, no one took us seriously as neutered non sectarians. So I managed to keep speaking without even mentioning his name. With a sardonic grin, he turned away, beckoned to the boys, and like a circus act leaving the ring they all trooped back into the bar to be rewarded, no doubt, with wee bags of Dolly Mixtures. George and I would meet again very soon, when he would make the Mid Ulster Election count the most remarkable ever, anywhere, anytime.

* * *

1964 THE PIGEON FANCIERS OF ULSTER

A few years before the "Troubles" broke out, the British government's Chinese Wall on Ulster cracked open when a brilliant, hard-nosed London reporter married a "lovely wee Irish nurse", both of them just beyond the first sweet bloom of youth. The reception, which I attended, was funny and festive in a Bishopsgate pub. For the honeymoon she proudly brought her husband home to Ireland where he just happened to spot a large council housing estate that was solely reserved for Protestant tenants only. His high scoop rating on the London news desk of The People, then the world's second-largest Sunday paper, brought dire warnings from the paper's Manchester news desk, which published the Irish editions. Manchester disliked unbalanced political stories about sectarian Ulster for the comical fear of upsetting a legion of mostly Protestant pigeon fanciers, a competition hobby greatly nurtured in that very plebian paper. Nobody can explain why Catholics were not duly bothered about pigeons. The Mancunian reservations were swept aside by London's appetite for a rattling good story, a poke in the traditional blind eye of Whitehall and the Commons. The tale was told across two pages. However many unionist pigeons lost their lofts, no one knows, but a much bigger door had flown open. It was almost certainly the first story of that kind in a British national paper since the distinguished essayist V.S. Pritchett was writing from Ireland for The Manchester Guardian in the 'Twenties. The Guardian, so sadly mistaken since, and a shadow of its former self, is now a cosy corner for the Sinm Fein IRA thuggery more lately invented in Derry and Belfast.

When the Prime Minister Douglas Home went along to the Palace on the last statutory day left to him in 1964 to ask the Queen to dissolve parliament and call an election, my wonderful wife Pamela Brooks, who married me for thirty years, was with me on the Mirror's business in Ireland. As a shy-at-first diplomat helping me to build bridges she was unpaid; there was always a culture of thrift at the Daily Mirror and its Sunday sister bordering on the abstemious. Pam was happy enough that our children's Nanny, Minnie Palmer, was awash in Mirror money instead. Minnie was happy too.

I was by then advising London that their first conception of a printing plant in Belfast to lead Irish publishing was the tail wagging the dog; the plant should be in Dublin alongside the larger editorial team, but my advice was lost on them. They were wary of printing in a foreign country, in spite of owning newspapers in Nigeria, so better the devil they thought they knew in Belfast UK. Another kind of devil was waiting. The Irish Republic, much like Norway and Belgium later on in those song contests, was a black hole in the Fleet Street of those years—Belgique nul points in the years to come.

A team of Manchester circulation men arrived to conduct advance trials. They were very soon cock-a-hoop at getting "dummies" printed in Belfast at 4.am, into Tralee, the county seat of Kerry, 300 rail miles plus central Dublin, by 8.30 a.m. "This is in good time" they chortled gleefully to London executives "to catch commuters coming into the city". Lockjaw was contagious around the table when I had to break the news that A) There were no commuters anywhere in Kerry in 1964 and B) Few paper shops throughout the South opened before 9.30 at the earliest—but most of them stayed open to near midnight to "catch home-bound commuters leaving early from the pubs". My Kerry cousin by marriage, Willie O'Connor, a publican, used to heave prone Saturday night customers out the door at 2.am with the warning: "Come on now John Joe, you'll be late for Mass". Well, I did offer the circulation department some encouragement; it was certainly true that Irish people, much more newspaper—literate than the British, would buy morning papers all day. When the DeValera-owned Irish Press Group cottoned on, they launched a big news-rich evening paper. It was unusually literate as well. The Evening Press became a pub-time favourite throughout the Republic and parts of the North; with a 100-mile head start on anything printed in Belfast. Even though the Dublin paper could not reach urban Kerry much before 5 p.m., it sold well, in competition with its sister morning paper, as well as the rival national and regional dailies. After the general election, I declined the editorship of the two Mirror nationals in Ireland, with Pam's relieved agreement. Our four school-age children, Averill, Shane, Conal and Fiona, with two tots, Catherine and Niall in waiting, were happy streamers in a parish primary and a convent grammar. Both schools were only yards from our five-bedroom Regency terrace house in timeless Bury St. Edmunds. In that beautiful ancient market town, a walker in Guildhall Street can inspect seven centuries of English urban architecture, about a third of it still residential. Family grocery bills at either of our two 18th century provision merchants were to be paid "on the nail" by the half-year, in April and October—sowing time and harvest time, see! Those would be around the times the farm subsidies arrived, and everyone in the town and in the "necklace" of villages around it, would have some extra money to spend. Every Wednesday and Saturday throughout the year the town bulges with the biggest one-day market in the country spreading its stalls around three streets. In the 1960s the Corn Exchange was still a grain bourse with weekly trading. On my first visit I was astounded to see an elderly Duke of Grafton, one of the regulars, sitting at a makeshift trestle table bartering with millers while sifting samples of his own corn from tiny snap-top brass and leather purses. Fearful of landing ourselves in debt beyond the normal, we managed to persuade the rival Co-Op, a 19th century upstart, to accept our cheques quarterly, and even that deal laid us open to traps of false prosperity.

The ignorance-based diktat of Mirror management that the whole exercise had to be located on Belfast would have made the school transfer too severe a change, especially for English children; I was proved right, a decade later, that it was a move still wrong, when without the protection of a substantial salary, just a freelance exchange of word with The Sunday Times to guarantee less than half my London-based £6000 with The Sunday Telegraph, I transferred the younger ones to Lurgan's Catholic parish schools, with disastrous results. Catholics yes, English no. The children were placed on the edge of things, and I had to protest. The parish priest, Mons Haughey, was nonplussed: A modestly poor man, he went about all day in a shabby soutane in the manner of a French rural cure. Slapping his sides by way of showing a despairing sympathy, he told me: "Mr. McGarvey! Anyone who puts English children into my schools is an idiot." He was sitting between two older men around a game of dominoes who just sat there grinning when he said it. Incredible to think of it now, Big-Head McGarvey (school nickname for physical and "head-case" reasons) was trying to save Ireland by stabilising the dying Northern Ireland Labour Party—but I am ahead of myself.

My refusal of the Mirror editorship in Ireland caused a tumult of surprise in the licensed gossip centres up and down the parish of St. Bride. Less to do with me, the buzz in the bars was caused by their second choice, my hoarse, crow-voiced wotcher-me-old-cock-sparrer Cockney-born picture editor on the Sunday Mirror, rarely ever out of London and never once in Ireland. The announcement had roughly the same shock value as Emperor Caligula's horse made Consul of Rome. It turned out, before the year was out, to be a stroke of genius and Derek Jameson, released from a glass-ceiling job, picture editors rarely promoted, was on his way to the highest pinnacles of editorship all round the bleedin' shop. I never once told him I had stepped aside, though he must have known that, The truth was, every step Jameson took confirmed my own view of myself; I couldn't edit a parish newsletter.

As for transferring English children to Belfast schools, and from Bury St. Edmunds, no thanks. Nearly two decades later a national TV programme adjudicated Bury as one of the twelve most desired residential towns in England. Manchester wasn't one of them, but wise-boy Derek had a simple answer. He persuaded the management to let him organise Ireland from there, giving his two boys the options of crackerjack schools. The schools in Northern Ireland later proved to be on a par with England's and often above when scales of performance were introduced.

From there, perhaps beguiled by the gap, he did preside over one single error of catastrophic proportions that I would more easily have blocked. An early "Irish" Daily Mirror did a two-page spread on, A Day in the Life of a B-Special, who by then were the part-time, fairly harmless auxiliaries to the RUC, the Junta's Protestant police force. Farm yokels and plumbers, they would patrol at danger spots, i.e Catholic areas, in ill-fitting hand-me-down uniforms with ankle-length greatcoats, wielding 303 Lee Enfield rifles to defend the Union for thirty bob a night—usually just the one night. Their original political raison d'terre was simply as an additional show of force to remind Catholics to stay in their place, resulting in their real status as scorned political bogeymen. There was no height reservation, short and portly no problem. Meeting them in the dark in their ankle-length great-coats gave you a strong impression of Russian infantry—circa 1917. The Mirror article had about the same effect as the fictitious musical on Broadway. Springtime For Hitler, would have had in Tel Aviv. Very soon after, the Mirror's £2m synchronised-to-Manchester printing plant, the first of its kind, went up in a Provo bomb that greatly shook the genteel suburb of Dunmurray.

Its residents, shaken and stirred to anger, were really much relieved to be rid of such a thing. A streak of uncharitable, unavoidable, *schadenfreude* crossed my breast at the news, having for totally different reasons advised that it should never have been there in the first place.

I endured a real stab of Jameson envy many years later, standing broke, jobless and wifeless on the traffic island footpath that runs down the centre of High Holborn. I was about to step off it when a dark blue Ford Granada limousine—stretched—swept round from Grays Inn Road, uniformed chauffeur in front, Derek enthroned behind. I stepped back and waved to him, but he had his head down in a forest of papers, on his way from a rail terminus to the top desk at the News of the World in Bouverie Street. Good ol' Derek, he sure had come a long way from van boy, tape-room messenger or whatever to this, and well-deserved. His low start to high promotion was once a Fleet Street norm, his career a Fleet Street classic. Uniquely on his way up, he remained well-liked. Derek was the right man.

And anyway, as I consoled myself, who ever heard of an Irish Catholic editing the News of the World! Derek left it years ago and made a new career for himself as a DJ on BBC Radio Two. He built a morning audience that rose to ten million at its peak. He died in September 2012, just a few months after his last paper was closed down by its owner in the heat of the phone-hacking scandal. In my professional life, he was my man for all reasons.

* * *

JUST ANOTHER DAY'S WORK.

In September 1965 Michael Christiansen, editor of The Sunday Mirror, who had never set foot in my family house, but had heard tales, accompanied the High Court Tipstaff to Dublin, and Ireland's High Court, to swear on oath that the safest place he knew of in either island for the care of a tug-of-love baby girl was the home of Paddy and Pamela McGarvey and their six young children in Bury St. Edmunds, Suffolk. Baby "F's" Scottish father had hidden her from her Australian mother in an Irish convent, and was languishing in a British prison for his contempt of court.

The deal worked. "F" was handed over to the Tipstaff, who in England handed her to me and I came home with about 30 other British and overseas journalists to see me hand a new baby to my wife, just as, more grist to this story, Pam was about to move a few doors away to the Bristol Wing of West Suffolk Hospital for the birth of her seventh child, our fourth son, also "F" Feargus we eventually decided.

Who won? As the law stands now I am not allowed to tell you, but her Scottish granny came out of the court smiling. And me, I took turns with Pam—honestly—changing the nappies of two babies.

CHAPTER TWELVE

The truant MPs

Novice Labour had two opponents, as I have related, a convicted bomber, Tom Mitchell, standing as Absentee Sinn Fein—meaning he would not attend parliament if elected—and the incumbent MP, George Forrest, who had barely attended parliament since elected, with only five recorded times in eight years. The seat, now smaller because the North has 17 Westminster seats, is yet again represented by an absenteee MP, Martin McGuinness no less, absent but salary earning with expenses at Westminster, where he will not take the oath, but is the Queen's Deputy First Minister to Peter Robinson at Stormont. I call this more Irish than the Irish themselves. More seriously, it is rank hypocrisy of the worst kind.

For all of its stony, fifty years the Stormont junta regarded their Westminster MPs seats as a sort of VIP Lounge, a Club Reserve to be used only when Ulster was threatened by any whisper of doubt from that temple of treachery. There was rarely any need for attendance in these calm 'Sixties, now that the wretched Irish Anti-Partition League, a mischief-making substitute for the Irish Party of yore, a nest of Labour vote catchers from Irish districts in Britain, was fading, its influence ebbing. Some Ulster Unionist members preferred permanent residence in the better environs of London W8, requiring only an urgent phone call from Belfast to pop down to the House for an hour or two.

George Forrest's long bouts of truancy were spotted by the most cruel parliamentary column in Fleet Street at the peak of its punching power, and the popularity of The Sunday Express which carried it. The paper then reigned supreme across the middle class. The Crossbencher column was conjured into life by a Canadian journalist invited to London by resident Canadian Max Aitken, Lord Beaverbrook, owner of the Express papers. The column began as an extension of his duties as Leader writer. Its style was marked by its short barking-dog sentences—just like that. One early theory held that Baxter was imitating the Beaver's own way of barracking his editors on the phone from his luxury apartment up behind The Ritz. *That story is no good. Bring that fellow back to the office. Tell him to write it again*—all in a growling, some would say snarling, Canadian accent pitched so low it would unnerve a Mountie's horse. Baxter was rewarded as Editor-in-Chief of the Daily Express (1929-33). After a period of freelancing, he entered parliament for the Tory seat of Southgate, later Wood Green, in 1950, retiring now in 1964, continuing in the very year a Crossbencher successor, the former Tory MP, George Clark, laid about my Ulster George in the unchanged Beverley Baxter style, barely a week or two before the end of the parliamentary term had to be called. Crossbencher demanded:

> *What strange unfamiliar voice rang out in the Commons last week?*
> *From the least familiar face in the commons?*
> *The face belongs to Mr. George Forrest, Unionist MP for Mid-Ulster.*
> *Mr. Forrest is seldom at Westminster. He rarely votes. He is never in the news.*
> *In eight years as an MP he has made just three speeches and asked two oral parliamentary questions.*
> *What deadly new peril for Ulster has brought Mr. Forrest hotfoot to Westminster?*
> *Why, nothing less than the Archbishop of Canterbury's Vestments Bill*

Then Crossbencher cleared his throat for his denunciation. Unfashionably, it was more than thirty words long.

> *Voters who are traditionally unionist have steadfastly returned a member of parliament who has almost as steadfastly remained at home, thus, in effect, giving Mid Ulster the sort of representation the Republicans promise—None.*

Forty years on, the shrivelled Mid-Ulster seat is still in that predicament. Fortunately I had read it just weeks before Pam and I unknowingly stepped into an extended Omagh council house—Phelim's—to tell them the Mirror's planned exposure of the town's dreadful housing situation was postponed, only to find the newly-socialised postmen in Phelim's group pre-programmed to catapult me into the election. I rang George Clark and got the Express Group's permission to publish Crossbencher on my Election Address. I omitted only the line about the Vestments bill, not wishing to tread on the sensitivity of Ulster parsons about those fellows in England garbing themselves on Sundays in colourful Papist mementos of imperial Rome. Many English clerics were long-time enthusiasts, the Archbishop merely trying to legalise it. It shook the sitting MP far more than I anticipated, as events would show. The Mid-Ulster seat has since been abandoned by Unionism ever since the 1969 result drew world-wide attention to the youngest MP, either gender, ever, just days before her 21st birthday. in the Commons, 20-year-old Bernadette Devlin, the bravest woman in Ireland. For a riot misdemeanour in Britain she would have been fined £15 and put on probation for throwing paving sets at policemen, if as severe as that—or today, a community-service sentence. Instead, the Ulster Junta's judiciary sent her to brutal, piss-pot Armagh prison for nine months. It was a political sentence.

On its exterior a handsome pre-Napoleonic edifice, dominating the east end of The Mall, it is a soul-chilling stone horror inside. I sat in one of the cells when the district council acquired it. Round about the same time, I shared Mrs. Bernadette McAliskey's fireside—(her teacher husband taught our youngest son Feargus for a year in St. Paul's School, Lurgan) distinctly warmer than her cell—in one enjoyable exchange of political views. We were very close save for my early conviction that the Republic must unreservedly recognise Northern Ireland, today only a half-way house with unstable Good Friday conditions, before we get to a situation enabling Billy McCool to marry Kathleen ni Houlihan for love or sensibility. The Republican Dream, like the American Dream, getting an over-ambitious Kathleen to abduct Billy from his unrecognised parents, is self-defeating. It has never worked in an Irish kitchen; it won't work anywhere.

THE END OF THE CAMPAIGN

Both Phelim and I—with our English wives and our Anglicised children, making us two of a kind, had determined that we should fight the election English-style. We had both absorbed and even experienced that element of fair play and decency so evident in England's shires, however questionable her conduct elsewhere. On the day itself I determined to tour the polling stations—smart suit, a dashing dark-brown Trilby hat, a Red rosette for Labour in my buttonhole, a rolled umbrella, brightly polished black Oxford laced shoes, and off I went. I was breaking ground yet again. Well, even the black shoes were a start in Ulster. The poll clerks delight at seeing me barely concealed their surprise at seeing me at all at all. No one else was bothering.

So on Thursday afternoon, October 15th 1964, polling day, I came to a primary school, approached by seven or eight steep steps, so that I did not see, until half-way up, about eight B-Men, uniform collars loose, tunics unbuttoned, squatting or lying full length on the granite paving between the steps and the door. Bright but waning sunshine was still warming the stones. An untidy assembly of empty bottles with familiar brown labels had already warmed the B-Men.

Their Lee Enfield 303s were stacked all round the porch, enabling them to cope unhindered with any untoward intrusion. In apparent command, seated on a bentwood chair, was a man in dark blue trousers and the Sam Brown jacket of an army officer of field rank—as likely a passed-over Major. The boys had got themselves a thirty-bob patrol to guard the polling station from a possible attack by hordes of angry Londonderry Fenians. The Major was earning maybe three pounds. His spliced uniform resembled the attire of the notorious Black and Tans, devised by Winston Churchill (as Lloyd George's War Minister 1919) and sent to Ireland "to introduce a short period of frightfullness" a request the Army had refused in 1916. He was sacked as the price the Tories demanded before joining Asquith's floundering Government. The prime minister asked him to hang around to keep an eye on Ireland, and when the Easter Rebellion imploded on them, Asquith would not permit him to accompany Kitchener, head of the army (and an absentee Kerry landowner) to Russia in July for an arms support conference. The Kitchiner conference ship struck a mine off Scotland and all were drowned. Just on 30 years later, World War Two ending, Churchill was universally recognised as the man who had saved the British from Nazi conquest. Did anyone ever mention Dublin Easter 1916? Of course not! Historians work mainly for their own countries. As I keep telling them, and some journalists, things happen because other things happened first.

So I stepped through them, and over them, muttering audibly: "Shocking, drunken rabble, disgraceful, court martial."

After my exchange of pleasantries with the polling staff, I emerged to another shock; the B men were up on their feet, buttoned up, standing-to with rifles at slope, the Major erect. They then presented arms in salute as I passed between them. In those reeling seconds, the traitor, the political turncoat, the Queen's McGarvey, could think only of my father, the honoured nationalist, Hibernian speaker, a long-time civic leader of Armagh, rolling in his grave as he beheld his wayward second son taking the salute from a gaggle of slutered B-Men. But as with the day of the Bad Confession in Armagh, all was well by the morn, on joining my Post Office supporters at the count in Omagh Town Hall the following morning. We socialist unionists all raised a greet cheer to the news that their hated Postmaster General, Reginald Bevins, had lost his seat in Lancashire. Not long after that delight, we were falling on the floor laughing, ribs aching with magical glee.

The B Men at the primary school reported to the presiding Under Sheriff their pride at standing to arms the day before in honour of the Lord Lieutenant. They seemed to be expecting some sort of official notice or reward. At that stage I knew that my well humoured father, a stage raconteur himself, had forgiven me.

The result for the United Kingdom's second largest constituency was expected about 3 p m. Long before that it was obvious that Forrest had retained his seat. At noon, he entered the auditorium and sauntered around the tables exchanging greetings with his party's count watchers. No one was expecting anything like his next move. Bounding up the side-steps to the stage, he strode across to the presiding Under Sheriff's Desk. Nelson Rowntree, by name almost certainly a Quaker, politely stood up to greet him, stepping back from his chair, whereupon Forrest, stride unbroken, used it as a stepping stone to the table, a wide, baize-covered combination of several. Two more strides brought him to the shaking front edge and the stacks of counted ballots, the Republican and Unionist votes towering over my quite respectable 5015, which, like the others, were elastic-bound in fifties.

Lashing out with his brown Chelsea boots, he kicked my bundles all over the hall, sending some of them flying for fifty or sixty feet. His boots were streaked with dung, indicating a morning visit to a Friday mart. I saw seated women struck full in the face and the back of their heads as the counting teams rose and hurried away to the walls on either side. Both men and women were displaying anxious signs of panic or disbelief and not least because, for added theatrics, the Hon member for Mid Ulster was screaming at the top of his voice, Yaroo, Yippee, Hurrah, Ya hah.

From the Sheriff's chair to the first kick, to the vote counters scrambling for safety, took less than seconds.

Standing, staring agape at all this I did not see the Under Sheriff until he grabbed me by the lapels of my jacket and, a much shorter man, propelled us into a corner of the stage. Shock led me to believe all of this was some sort of Protestant treason and plot to discredit me, **So you think you're a Unionist—Croppy Lie Down, and** here was the Presiding Officer at it—his teeth chattering, his normally pale complexion now parchment white, this is what he said; I have never forgotten it.

"Mr. McGarvey" and he drew his breath deeply, "Mr. McGarvey, I am a unionist but I know your day will come. I just know that. Your day WILL come"

When he had exhausted the hundred bundles of my ballots, our MP, smirking and swaggering, found himself trapped on the table, unwilling to trust his bulk to a rickety bentwood chair on the way down. Supporters rushed to help him, while the vote counters were scrambling under tables looking for my votes. He began to speak to Rowntree, but was cut short with the Under Sheriff's pointed arm gesture to the exit steps. He turned away with a sly sidelong grin at me. A farm boy surely still, I thought again.

I made no complaint. With the Under Sheriff on my side there was no need to, and it was him who raised the storm. For the first time in its history, a sitting MP was expelled from the Unionist Party, though, as I recall, some other misconduct was quoted as the reason. The Mid-Ulster result having been legally blackballed so many times perhaps they feared another if his behaviour at the count was cited. It was all much ado; when the matter came up before the Ulster Unionist Council, a body of several hundred Protestants constantly pre-conditioned to say NO, the Party was briskly told to reinstate him; there was to be no breach in the impregnable defence of Fortress Ulster.

George Forrest, with this benchmark of behaviour, was just like all the other dogged bigots. The Ulster Unionists were still an integral branch of the Conservative Party. His actions carried a clear message to me, Croppy Lie Down, for that's who you are, and don't dare come anyway near us pretending you're a Unionist.

The greatest weakness in the defence of Ulster was the maxim that only Protestants were allowed to be the defenders.

And yet, in Forrest's case, I and many others might have misunderstood him, either that or he had a Damascene conversion of sorts. Only three years later, expressing support for the "Lundy" Prime Minister, Terence O'Neill, *that treacherous host to that Taoiseach fellow Lemass from the Republic*, and *entertaining bloody Fenian nuns to tea*—ergo a man trying to instil some political sanity to the place—poor George was dragged from a unionist platform by a howling crowd of "Orange Defenders". Thrown to the ground, he was beaten and kicked unconscious. He held the seat until his untimely death in 1969, when his widow, Anna, nominated but declining to campaign, was defeated by the pixieish Bernadette. Because she stood mid-way as a Unity candidate, some commentators said I had marked her path in declining the traditional Catholic political route, but that was reason stretched too far. Bernadette remained a nationalist.

The future Mrs.McAliskey was a campaigning fireball driven by her own steam to win Mid—Ulster whatever had gone before. For a novice MP especially, to cross the floor of the Commons and pummel the paunch of a cabinet minister was merely a reflection of the frustration established by the permanent paunches of the Unionist Junta, towards which Home Secretary Reggie Maudling, his predecessors and successors, continually turned a blind eye.

Only Bernadette could have done that, armoured with a schoolgirl rage. I had declined a nomination to the short lists of two English constituencies, South Cambridge and Eton and Slough, in order to make the stand for change where it was most needed, and to that extent I succeeded—5015 votes, even though the enormous percentages of Mid—Ulster left me, still today, the UK's most popular deposit loser. I take additional consolation observing the experience of others; journalists make poor, sometimes even lousy members of parliament. When asked why, I put it like this: Journalist MP: "Look. There is a huge hole in the road. We cant go on. We must stop and mend it." Non-journalist MP: "Nonsense, we can walk around it.

* * *

AN APPLE A DAY

My native city of Armagh, more than a century older than Canterbury, as I perforce often advise unworldly English friends, nestles below an arcade of orchards stretching for thirteen miles from east to west and six miles in depth, hence its all-Ireland map reference as, The Orchard County. Hard and shiny light green apples flourish under names such as Grenadier and Ladyfinger, but if you are eating a Mr. Kipling Apple Pie with your afternoon tea, ten to one it is filled to the brim with Armagh Bramley. The big, uneven apple, a delight from the oven after the Sunday roast, cored, coddled and stuffed with raisins, was awarded territorial exclusivity in origin by Brussels in 2012 (They did not insist on levelling the bumps)

In a lovely glade near Loughgall one fine late summer's day in 1974, Pam and I were standing in the garden of a handsome Regency farmhouse we were considering buying for the five of our seven children accompanying us to Northern Ireland. The house was big enough, and primly Protestant, but offset by the lack of space in the rooms, and it was more than five miles from the city's schools. But the garden's beautiful layout, with pretty shrubs and seven apple trees, was still holding my English wife's interest and the owner's son noticed. A man of middle years, he walked over to the nearest tree, plucked a blushing specimen, and slicing it deftly with a penknife, proffered her the famous English dessert apple she easily recognised by the tiny red veins in the flesh. She was exclaiming her delight, "Oh it's a . . ." but your man had beaten her to it. "There you are Mrs McGarvey", he declared proudly, "Blood of the Boyne"

"And they call themselves British" she exclaimed on our way back to the city. (Her Church of England ire was up) "Fancy doing that to a poor little Beauty of Bath". I reminded her of the case of apples I brought back to Suffolk the previous September, after I pulled up at an orchard gate near Moy. The grower had shown me a bright green apple in his store with the warning; "You see that apple there" he said, "Well that is a good cooker for now. But if you keep that apple to Christmas, it will turn as yella as a duck's foot, and it will be a dessert apple." Marvelling, I told him I must tell my wife its name. He looked anxiously up and down the road before turning to me with a sly grin, "Them apples Paddy, is No Surrender."

An apple a day keeps Catholics away?

* * *

CHAPTER THIRTEEN

The Tale of Trilby

Michael Wells, late of the army and some military intelligence with the Ox and Bucks Light Infantry, a much favoured regiment in its day (his wife, Elsie, a matron-of-honour at our first civil marriage) was, as this canine tale begins, a senior export executive of a huge British milling combine. It began on a Monday morning, never the best time for the unexpected. His PA arrived for work, but all mumsy and giggling as she produced the reason, a struggling, wriggly puppy she plopped on his desk.

"There" she exclaimed with a burst of relief. "What are we going to do with this wee laddie? Before he could answer, he could tell right away his PA was not versed in the obvious clues to animal gender. Pausing only to pee in the manner of a wee lassie, and all over Wells's leather-framed FT Calendar Desk Pad 1967, she leapt into space and spread-eagled herself a good six feet away from the desk. A rapid recovery sent her scudding along the corridor of offices in RHM's Glasgow headquarters, feminine squeals of delight and horror as pleasures were reduced to the shocks of some torn tights, a fashion novelty to boot. Eventually recaptured, explanations beginning, the pup was placed for its own safety in a huge hamper provided by the mail room—another mistake. This rather exceptional minor canine leapt twice its own height to the edge of the basket, knocked it over and sped away again. Next time a big lid was loosely applied as a deterrent. Though presumably born in Scotland, some thought this was something of a transfer, an English Springer Spaniel in its infant embryo. "Aye, right enough, that's what the policeman said it was" PA ventured over her first relieving cigarette. "That must be why it's jumping up and down all the time.

"Yes, I did notice that" mused her English boss from Military Intelligence Six. He set out to extract from her the origins and reasons of the sudden appearance of a puppy in the august senior management environs of Rank Hovis McDougall. It was wandering, lost, with no collar, near her flat when returning home from the great celebrations which burst out all over the real capital of Scotland within minutes of a final whistle blown in faraway Lisbon which gave Glasgow Celtic undisputed possession of the European Cup. Emblazoned all over the city in electric headlines and bare graffitl were the magic numbers—Celtic 2 Inter Milan 1. In some parts of the city the celebrations could still be heard. It was nothing as simple as mere victory, it was a first for any British team. It was a Scottish triumph over those banana-heads in England, Scotland's glory won with a Scottish football caber up the English posterior. And so, the police told PA she should keep the pup. Her boss also told her to keep it. She couldn't. The poor wee thing would have to be locked up all day, and besides, she argued, didn't he have children, and so why didn't he take it home, which he did and very soon after that he left for London with family and Trilby to buy a minimarket store in Hanwell.

Trilby? A name for a dog? Captain Wells patiently explained to questioners, something about remembering literary heroine Trilby's link with a wild Scottish imp. He was a good trend spotter, at least for selling food and feed if not naming pups. The age of the supermarket had dawned. The Hanwell shop prospered twice beyond its size. The second extension tore away the staircase to the flat above, reached only by a fire-escape from the yard. Trilby was isolated all day, the hardworking parents below, the children at school. A new owner had to be found.

This old friend with a large family in a dinky Regency town house in far off Bury St. Edmunds, the one that cost only £2000, from which, selling it for £3000 ten years later, they were about to move to a small five-bedroom manor in south Bucks. It was in the outskirts of Slough "The Home of Horlicks," auctioned at £7,500. Now also a wistful memory, and with a half acre of gardens, it altogether seemed the ideal solution for Trilby as well. The deal was done after a few trial "walkies" in Hanwell Park. On the hundred mile drive to Suffolk in the Morris Oxford Estate her new owner paused on a long stretch of the A505 where grass-centred side lanes—in Ireland "boreens"—rose up on to Royston Downs, the northern geological match of the ones he long ago encountered, in Sussex. Heart-in-mouth, he released the cooped up spaniel, by now a boisterous four-year-old, on to the chalky slopes where famed steeplechasers had trained. Trilby took off in a wide circle, a slipstream of fine chalky dust rising behind her. To his immense relief she turned right back towards him. The walking days in Hanwell Park had worked. Both celebrated with a good piddle far enough away from the road not to offend. They resumed their seats in the car, the Springer with the characteristic leap few other breeds can match.

The real test of ownership was to come. Madam—who would become Mistress—was uncertain at the timing, and anxious at the trouble a new adult dog might cause in a household of seven children expecting to move house. At the front door he edged the car on to the pavement to block any chance of a mad dash up the street, opening the two nearside car doors for added safety. Madam opened the front door of the house to a rocket skidding along the front hall's ancient tiles, all the way to the kitchen, back again and up the enclosed staircase to the bedrooms, and then we heard skidding and sliding on extended claws over the bathroom's plastic floor, before she came tumbling down again to the carpets of the knock-thru living room.

It's a family memory still, the house filling up with gossamer clouds of Royston chalk. Mistress, after seven children which, she maintained, "was just like podding peas" was a tomboyishly beautiful lady, her face alien to powder or paint, did not escape. Her welcoming countenance creased into a Gothic laugh. The new arrival came to a panting rest at her feet, chin up, head cocking left, and then right, with the direct wide-eyed query only this breed can muster with unmistakeable clarity across the species. *Who are you? Am I yours? Are you mine?* There could no doubt about the answers.

This is a breed that demands human companionship, says Tanya B Ditto in her manual* on the Springer, *"friendly, loyal and eager to please"* and adding, *"with a competitive spirit capable of earning honours in the field, in the show ring, and in your heart."*

For the Scottish English Springer it was third owner lucky. It was the beginning of a long love affair that would stretch for nearly a decade into the life of a young family growing up within the bonding that she provided. The bond was never more evident than during family holidays at an old toll house on the river Thames, where once upon a time, on foot, on cart or coach wheels, or just on your horse, you paid a fee to cross the bridge between Oxfordshire and Berkshire. The river here flows under it in a slight dog-leg curve (so it has to be said). Paddling shallows on one side, safe for children, extended upstream to just-as-safe breast height for adult swimmers.

A little further up, a famous Irish-born author-Don and her husband were often two of them, naked to the embracing river. The tollhouse was on the Berkshire side and shared two levels between the road and a lawn that bore a boathouse for punts, alongside sites for visitors bringing their own caravans. All of this was a blissful childhood haven for Mistress in summer holidays not far removed from Swall*ows and Amazons*. She had her own clinker-built dinghy, measured for her in the other roadside boatshed operated by her Uncle Dick, and from which she led her own gangs of Famous Fives, local children and visitors', in real riverside adventures. One side of her boat, sawn in half from bow to stern, for years propped up a bar in the pub immortalised by Jerome J. Jerome just a few yards further up the same bank.

And of course, Jerome too had a dog. Montmorency could not have had the same fun as Trilby. The *Three men in a Boat* stayed only one night at the Barley Mow, nothing like Trilby's summer and autumn treats. For her spaniel vibes a holiday by a river had to be bliss. As soon as she saw Mistress on the paddling shallows with the children, throwing off a beach coat to go swimming, the dog ran ahead to a grassy headland closer to the bridge. From there, tail thrumming, she watched her idol breast the flow and swimming towards her. Only then would she take the action that had the children shrieking with delight, a leaping great swoosh from bank to stream to join her. Why the dog never waded into the water beside her was something of a mystery, unless it had to be that instinct for leaping.

The relationship was now part of a mystique that seemed to keep the whole family intact and involved with her, the shiny wet muzzle resting in the lap of a crying child could dry tears with one magical full-stop sob. Her eyes, brown and so visible, so typical of the breed, the bitch especially, seemed to radiate every human emotion. Under the bridge and back again the pair swam together, sometimes side by side, other times in line, and on some days with Mistress's doppelganger cousin from the old toll house, who, t'was avowed by awed male locals, swam *au naturale* there at dawn, the whole year round. Them 'boys' all solemnly reckoned this to each other in the Barley's mature tap room. Somehow, none of the tap room ever seemed to make the riverbank at dawn. And besides, Cousin had her own swimming companion, a gander called Henry, but when the spaniel was in the river, Henry discreetly stayed on the other side where he had lots of reeds to root. And then the blow came. Glasgow Celtic celebrated the tenth anniversary of the Big Win. It was all in the papers again, with bits on southern telly. Lady Kelly, as she now was, wife of club chairman Sir Bob, recalling her only downside to those memorable days, the sad loss from her car of a beautiful English Springer Spaniel pup. It just jumped out and ran away. All nine people in Trilby's family were stunned. Should we tell the Kellys these ten years later? Surely we must. The journalist in the family thought we must; what a story for his paper. He was out-voted by an emotional ballot of eight to one, as well as some neighbours joining in. Even in the unlikely event Lady Kelly would demand her return, a sort of canine cowardice prevailed. The score this time; Our Trilby 9 Glasgow Celtic 0. A fourth referee in the stands might have cried foul. Only a few years later, after the club had changed hands, no one working there could trace any whereabouts of the Kelly family.

Eventually our association would have to have an ending, but not yet. It would obviously be sad, but also something of a miracle, even sensational some would say. Master became involved in what would become the peace process of Northern Ireland and the whole family, all but the two eldest children now setting out on their own careers, moved from idyllic leafy Bucks to ghetto-scarred Lurgan. The divisions were hard on some of the children. Mistress expecting tradesmen saying they would be there "this evening" found them at the front door after lunch. Trilby merely swapped England's most iconic river for a gallop in the shallows of Ireland's largest lake, Lough Neagh. On family drives up the coast road above Belfast the Mull of Kintyre would come first to view across St. George's Channel and the children would tease her; "Look Trilby, there's your country."

Nearer home, the shore of the Lough, which was forming a natural leisure area for the expanding new city of Craigavon, was now her playground, Mistress firmly resisted the temptation to pick the wild orchids hiding in the green grassy slopes at the water's edge. The dog was now nearly ten years at the family's heart and obviously broaching 14. Her body thickened as her exuberance for walking and swimming ebbed. A small fortune was spent with a conscientious young vet trying to stave off the inevitable. When a likely day came and he could do no more he quietly said so. He told Mistress he had all the facilities ready at his surgery. And that would have been that, this story never told, beyond a name and a family memory. But it was no deal. Mistresss told him to come to the house instead. Her swimming companion would be buried in her garden. The house at Lurgan stood on its own ground. It was built by a Lord Lurgan for his estate secretary early in the 19th century. The sloping rear garden rose again towards the playground of a convent school and the yards of a nylon spinning mill, built with business vigour in the 'Fifties and closed again in the nylon-swamped 'Sixties, In its latest role it was an army "sangar," which, says the OED, is a fortified round hollow. This "hollow" was five stories high.

A Royal Stuart tartan car rug was found, a hangover from the years only a few cars had optional heaters. It was laid on the kitchen floor just under the garden window. The Scottish rug was just a coincidence, yet nothing finer was as fitting for her shroud. Eyes brimming, Mistress held her still and gently stroked her grey muzzle as the vet prepared the needle. Eldest son had arrived from London for this unavoidable event and in Master's unavoidable absence, carried her body down the garden to where a younger brother was digging a grave. Very, very suddenly, and in a manner so sudden as frightening, the two young Englishmen were confronted by armed soldiers shouting at them to desist, to put down the parcel, to stand back, with hands up. Behind them more soldiers were clambering over the hedges and wires that formed the loose boundary between the garden and the army post. An officer barely weeks older than Eldest Son beckoned a sergeant to examine the bundle. The soldiers lowered their guns. The "squaddies" serving in Northern Ireland had a habit of adopting stray dogs, often keeping them as mascots. More than one abandoned Ulster mongrel found itself in the London tabloids as evidence of our tender-hearted teenage troops. The silence in the garden was broken by a cry from one of them. "Ouch, it's only a poor wee Scottish dog." The tartan had eased away the tensions of their first approach. Shane looked around them alerted by the accent. They were all Scots, and mixed. Some had pom-poms on their caps, others sporting glengarrys rimmed with red and white chequer.

Their next step was unanimous, inevitable, unspoken, unordered. They gathered in military formation on either side of the grave. Members of two Scottish regiments formed a guard of honour in Ireland over the grave of the English Springer Spaniel Glasgow Celtic lost the weekend they conquered Europe. Trilby's wheel of life had turned full circle. Were any of the soldiers Celtic supporters? Nobody asked. With two regiments some might have been Rangers men. At such an event as this nobody cared. In well trained unison, they raised their guns in the air and mouthed pum-pom noises over the grave. Back at the kitchen window Mistress forced a smile through her tears. Short of a lone piper playing The Flowers of the Forest, Scotland's royal lament, she could have had no finer farewell. In County Down another Springer was found. Her name was Tolly, making oddly, another football connection with Tollemache, the brewery family that then owned Ipswich Town. Not long afterwards, Master and Mistress returned separately to England.

***The English Springer Spaniel, by Tanya B. Ditto—Barron**

CHAPTER FOURTEEN

1984 A Cabinet Minister On Ice

I was foot-free, unemployed and wandering loose from a boarding house in Suffolk. I was on my own. Pam had divorced me in Ulster's High Court. Our children asked me not to defend it. They were first to make the announcement. "Mammy wants to be herself" I was told as the only reason she gave. I did not defend it. There are no more details here because they are not all mine to explain.

The road distance from Bury St. Edmunds to Brampton, both in Suffolk, is a surprising 55 miles, with still a few more winding wolds to spare eastwards to the shingly shores of the North Sea. Most of the tar-and-chip route was still 19th-century narrow, winding and replete with frightening road camber tilted against the bends instead of coaxing your vehicle around them. An imperative early morning start for a midday appointment was made more hazardous by a New Year frost riming the hedges and black-icing the narrow twisting road. I remember thinking of Chesterton's sally as—the rolling English drunkard *froze* the rolling English road. The BBC's weather forecast warned motorists not to venture out. But there could be no cancellation, no turning back. Waiting for me at the other end at a very high noon for me was a chance, as slim as it was unexpected, to change the tortured history of Britain and Ireland, for the better, and possibly forever. My destination was an easily found moated farmhouse. The moat, a surprise in the first week of January, was dry, a point of some political irony for its owner, denounced by an angry Prime Minister as one of her "wets". On a wide greensward bordering the moat and the house, three policemen wearing side-arms directed me to park. Two of the three police cars were freshly dented front and back, evidently from the same skating shunt. I could not resist a private snigger at my own driving prowess against their's, mine made easier by a cheap, much derided and badly underrated car with front-wheel drive and a wheel mounted on each corner, virtually impossible to skid or overturn, my third Austin Maxi.

Two of them checked my credentials while the other spoke to the household on a brick-sized mobile phone, or maybe it was a two-way radio. The East Suffolk constables were noticeably wary of my Ulster accent, exchanging glances as I spoke, hardly surprising considering their role and location. The rolling wolds are little different from Ulster's drumlins, especially those in Co. Down, but Ulster voices in East Suffolk?—I might just as well have been a Laplander left behind from Christmas. (with a sleigh that worked) As I crossed the moat and walked up the short path, James Prior, MP, Her Majesty's Secretary of State for Northern Ireland, was standing at his front door.

Centred on a fork in the Gt. Yarmouth road leaving Bury St. Edmunds, stands a handsome double fronted Victorian house. It was then the home of the notable Guardian columnist, the late Hugo Young, a Balliol College law graduate who had unexpectedly turned to journalism, coincidental to the election of a woman as leader of the Conservative Party. She was the first gender breach in a long line of males since Walpole invented the role. This was clearly so sharp a change in British politics he began taking and retaining notes for what became his searching biography of Margaret Thatcher, **One of Us** (Macmillan '89)*. Perhaps even then he was scribbling some notes as I drove past his window. I have to say here that I won the in-office Sunday Telegraph leadership sweep, choosing her amid ribald cries of lunacy, meaning me as well, my prize so small I have forgotten how much. Young described, with rare Guardian accuracy, the senior British cabinet minister now leading me into his house.

'Prior was a genial fellow, and cleverer than he looked. In appearance he was the acme of a Conservative farmer, the vocation he pursued, along with many business interests, supported by a first class degree from Cambridge in estate management. He had an engaging honesty about him, and a decent gallantry. He took some time to master his incredulity that Margaret Thatcher was now his leader, but sniped at her behind her back far less cruelly than some other colleagues on the left of the party.'

*PAN MACMILLAN copyright permission.

Thatcher, in turn, was disappointed in him. She placed him in the firing line of her industrial reforms, to tame the union barons by reducing their influence inside and outside 10 Downing Street. She also wanted him to stop industry-related unions supporting each other in strikes, a policy that would bring Britain to the brink of serious civil unrest as the miners struggled man to man on public roads with police under orders to stop their "flying pickets" going from strike to strike.

As Secretary of State for Employment, his methods were seen as balanced, much too soft for her. If you were not on the right and right beside her, you were not "one of us"—you were one of her "wets". By then the wretched Ulster nuisance job was usually apportioned to *arriviste* lightweights on the way up, or even just attaining the rank that had to go with the job, as well as a Cabinet chair, but from which you could return rewarded for a brave try with the Home Office or Defence, as some did, Tory as well as Labour.

Sending so senior a Tory heavyweight to Belfast was widely seen as banishment intended as punishment. In army terms he would readily recognise, he was on "jankers", but the punishing regime he adopted in Ulster with the noticeable companionship of his wife Jane as a virtual Proconsul or First Lady, charmed the province to a degree not previously known there. Ladies in macho political Ulster were mostly "told" to stay at home. Between the appointment and his arrival, a clerical Ulster MP was murdered by terrorists in London. When Her Majesty's Secretary of State arrived in loyalist Ulster to attend the funeral as his first visible duty there, he was beaten round the back and legs by umbrella-wielding Unionists. There were no arrests; he had not been molested by Catholics.

Jim Prior's easy geniality is catching, as Ulster folk of either ilk soon found. We shook hands on his doorstep. I was still marvelling my luck. I was a private citizen, not even an employed journalist. The soaring chance that this wholly unexpected meeting offered had virtually dissolved the aftermath miasma of my divorce a year before. Just to meet here, at this time, in this place, arranged within moments after we met, was a clear pointer to the orthodoxy of what I was attempting. It was also very much a very Irish situation.

A MAGIC CHRISTMAS CARD

Flashback—by a few weeks to late November 1983, and a commercial Christmas party in Ulster House, Northern Ireland's "embassy" and trade centre in Berkeley Street, Mayfair. My visit was random look-see—nothing much else to do. The industrialist Sir Desmond Lorimer was about to switch on festive lights around a display of north Irish Christmas goodies ranging from linens to dairy produce, and Beleek's unique chinaware, hence the dim lighting prevailing as I shuffled in amongst those standing at the back. Three very tall men, Finn McCool types you might say, also latecomers, stood alongside me. The one furthest away leaned across the other two with extended hand: "Hullo there, I'm Jack Antrim and I'm a linen-master, which is why *I'm* here.

The one in the middle followed suit, having read my large lapel ID card: "How d'do Mr. McGarvey. I'm Aubrey Downshire and I'm another linen-master, and that's what has *me* here"

And "Daddy Bear", the tallest one next to me? A strangely familiar voice came down past the hairs on my neck as they jumped up to tingling attention "I'm afraid I'm *not* a linen-master, *I'm* just Terence O'Neill."

Well, inside or outside frontline journalism, it's not every day, and off days especially, you're head and shoulders with a former Prime Minister—my head, his shoulders. O'Neill served the war a Captain in the Irish Guards. I have used italics, and pseudonyms, in their introductions to illustrate here the cautious, sly-boots Ulster argot of asking you virtually everything about yourself by telling you very little. And so in cautious response I told all three: "*I'm just going around talking to people about forming a research group to look for an Ulster solution—one idea is a neutral parliamentary capital, something like Ottawa, Canberra.*"

The linen-masters tilted their heads at me with tilted grins, the unspoken but polite Ulster way of saying *You're the quare boy right enough*. The man Ian Paisley tore from office for daring to have tea in a Catholic school with a nun-headmistress, well, he pulled a moue on his lips before saying: "Well, that's a tall one."

Dark glances were visible in the gloom around us—Sir Desmond still speaking—and we were "shushed" by our neighbours. A commotion at the rear indicated the arrival of someone important. A sharp dig in my ribs—we were still in an electric twilight. Lord O'Neill of the Maine he was now. Half whispering, yet audible again to several, he said: 'the Secretary of State has just come in. You're better off giving him that idea of yours than to me because he's a far more important man now than I ever was'

James Prior, an armed guard on either side, had heard what he was meant to hear, grinning as I turned round. Fourteen years before Tony Blair discovered the "hand of history" I felt the hand of "O'Neill Himself" as the Middle Irish would have addressed the main man, usurper family or real. Guiding mine, delivered by that dig in the ribs.

Over my head (five foot nine) the Norfolk Regiment shook hands with the Irish Guards. Prior slipped a card to me from a well tailored waistcoat, murmuring : "Ring Jane after Christmas." I did, and she said: "He has flu" I audibly sagged at the old political saw. She said: "No no, it's not like that, he really wants to see you. Ring again"

Over the previous three years Jane Prior had worked ameliorating magic in Ulster's troubles. She was the first British Proconsul wife that we know of to make any First Lady movements on the tattered, unsociable province, going everywhere her presence was needed and useful. I did as she asked and so here I am, me myself with the Secretary of State to myself.

He led me through to a huge conservatory, so large it seemed out of kilter with the house. It was like the atrium of a seaside hotel, set with tables and chairs. I cottoned on it was this Tribune's room for his followers for anything from bingo to bargain sales, indoors for the Tory Fete if wet—that word again. I have no detailed memory of the conversation which lasted forty minutes; I was doing the talking for a change, the Cabinet minister making notes, the while a North Sea wind playing on the glass walls was slowly solidifying my knees.

I do remember the relief when we reached the blissful warmth of the kitchen to say hello and goodbye—and thanks—to Mrs. Prior. She was standing by an old fashioned farmhouse black range, just like the one up which my stressed mother fired my sawdust-leaking doll, Molly. It felt hot enough to drive our "Wee Local" train from Armagh to Portadown but was merely awaiting the two dressed pheasants sitting on the table.

A month later he wrote from his Whitehall office, February 8, 1984. I reproduce it here in full for three reasons. Although it rejects the neutral parliamentary capital, the sweep of the letter teeters on the brink of accepting it. He was also intrigued by the idea, and he is confirming there is no constitutional bar to it in either part of Ireland. In fact, it is clearly seen in the first constitutions contained in the 1920 Better Government of Ireland Act, the Bell, Book and Candle of both Irelands.

Public acceptance, unlikely then as he emphasises repeatedly, in fact his only reason for rejection, is now demonstrably more pliable amid the middle-class opinion formers; while the "war" continues in the streets. The sectarian walls have been reinforced, heightened, and extended. Bigotry is maintained by the kind of people dictator Juan Peron of Argentina used to call "my shirtless ones"—Protestant defenders who rarely go near any church. Above all else, it is quite clear in the letter that Jim Prior liked the idea.

In Stormont. A 2011 poll has revealed a Catholic majority in favour of staying in the union

"Dear Mr. McGarvey

I was glad to meet you to discuss your ideas about a shared parliamentary capital for Ireland and to look at the papers you lent me, and which I now return. I also have your letter to my Private Secretary of 18 January.

"Thanks to the helpful exposition of your scheme when we met and in the various papers I now have a clear idea of what you propose. *The scheme is challenging in its departure from all the conventional ways of thinking about institutions for resolving the difficulties in Northern Ireland*, (my italics) but having thought about it with some care, I am afraid I have to conclude that it is not something the Government could support.

As my private Secretary said in his letter of 11 January, in the Government's view proposals for the resumption of devolved government in Northern Ireland must enjoy widespread support, that is support in both parts of the community, in Northern Ireland. (This is not very far away from the objective set out in Brian Faulkner's book you attach to your most recent letter) Not only do we think this criterion is absolutely right in principle in Northern Ireland's circumstances; we also think the ample evidence of history shows that no scheme failing to meet it will offer the likelihood of stable and effective government. Thinking back on all I have learned in the past three years about the attitudes of the politicians, and those they represent, on each side of the community in Northern Ireland, I doubt whether your scheme would meet that condition. Indeed I think it would be counter-productive, if I were to float it. Unionists would be deeply and irreconcilably suspicious of a proposal for an Assembly or a parliament sited outside Northern Ireland.

"I know that in putting forward your proposals you are moved by a sincere concern to see the resolution of the problem of Northern Ireland. *If we thought that there was a real prospect that a plan such as yours would command cross-community support we would take it very seriously indeed.* But I hope you will understand that I do not feel it would commend widespread acceptance throughout the community."

The last paragraph, like his personal signature, was in his own handwriting: "Sorry to be such a "wet blanket" but I don't see your plan as a way forward at the moment."

His letter was the beacon that finally fired my half-formed ideas into the foundation of an independent research engine (I invented that concept before Microsoft) to seek a solution overseas. Various doors opened to me when I sought help and a common consensus directed me to consult an oracle at Oxford.

Many times long since I have referred back to Jim Prior's central view outlined twice in my italics. That time—"*cross community acceptance*" has long since arrived, if we are to judge by the "chuckle brothers" alliances.

CHAPTER FIFTEEN

My One Day at Balliol

The college, I was constantly reminded, perhaps not quite true unless you considered the foreigners, had produced more prime ministers than any other of its kind, almost as if it had done little else in Oxford. Balliol men were said to be exceptional in the width and depth of their approach to things. I recognised the bluff sand-coloured building as the most obvious college in the city centre. I recalled tears of deprivation astride an illicit motorbike at the traffic lights in St. Giles, on that marathon across England to see again my Shropshire Lass, way, way back in 1949. (Well, I impressed her parents) Funny that, I can remember it while unable to remember who sent me to Balliol for advice on setting up a research charity on Ireland's muddled constitutions.

Now seeing it again, I was near blubbing again, a feeling this time that parts of my life had been wasted. The most oversubscribed college for entry, its political ambience is to the left, which would have suited me fine. I might have been more at home with the culture expressed by that lazy old dog of a Prime Minister, Asquith, looking back on his college, as having acquired "the tranquil consciousness of an effortless superiority." Presiding over Britain's worst period of mass slaughter of her sons at war, he wrote daily to an eleven-year-old girl, Venetia Stanley, until her audulthood. My father's coaching on manners would have had something to say about that. Another strange aspect,—the college keeps tortoises in its gardens. An undergraduate gets delegated year by year as Keeper. Had I known, I would have regaled the Master about my tortoise. (A good thing wee Eddie Branken and his Lurcher never got to Balliol either).

The Master then, 1984, also had a tale to tell, for a play, a film as likely. Dr.Anthony Kenny, knighted since our meeting, is a philosopher who has specialised in analytical Thomism (so I am told) which relates to the theory that it can be adopted to a more Aquinas-led application to the problems of modern life. As they are talking about the same philosopher, I took this to mean that St. Thomas Acquinas was a split personality, and left it at that. Sir Anthony has more degrees than a temperature gauge, certainly more honours and awards than can be recounted here. They begin with graduation from the Venerable English College in Rome, followed by ordination as a curate to serve in the earthy parishes of Liverpool—Father Anthony John Patrick Kenny, so no doubt whatever as to his ethnic origins, and then the sheer astonishment of his transformation, from there to up here., Balliol, Master of. He had inner doubts in doctrine—then came his self-laicisation, a declared atheist but still bound to his vows of celibacy, so it was his subsequent marriage brought excommunication, if that had not previously happened "in the breast". Although he has not returned to Holy Church, holy churchmen still recognise his worth, more lustre added long since by the Aquinas Society of America. I detected no side with him, no pomposity. A Dominican friar I broached in Cambridge about him only recently exclaimed: "Oh, you mean Tony Kenny." It all sounded very much as if he was still in the fold.

He met me at Masters Lodge, which stands on the north side of Broad Street cornering into St. Giles, noticeable from there for the distinctive oriel window which hangs over the street like the rear gunner's capsule in a B2 bomber. I was led upstairs to an enormous "events" room on the first floor, passing, on the staircase, a larger-than-life portrait of a cardinal in flowing scarlet. As we sat in faded armchairs about twenty foot apart on a carpet of visible threads, Dr. Kenny listened intently to my tales and aspiration to solve the Irish Question by the same means with which so many other countries had solved it for themselves. His most memorable advice was that I should not write a book on Anglo-Irish constitutions because nobody would read it, advice I accepted with the relish you'd expect from a hotshot tabloid hack accustomed to shooting forty lines for eleven million readers. So here it is, as you read it now around my misadventures in life and work. That's how you've been tricked into reading this one after you enjoy reading all about my jokey occupation as a journalist.

Anthony Kenny warmly approved of my idea for a dedicated think tank, charity based, for Ireland's problems. As I stood to leave, and we were nearing the door, he took me by the sleeve, back across the room to the oriel window. From the street we most likely appeared as a pair of tailor's dummies. The effect was dizzying and I was glad he was still holding my sleeve. Pointing down to a darker patch on the street's blue-grey macadam, enclosed in a narrow iron ring, he asked. "Do you know what that is?

I didn't, venturing it was obviously not a manhole; there was no sign of a handle

"That is where we burned Cranmer" he told me matter-of-factly, as though "we" had done it only yesterday. At least subconsciously, that "we" meant us Catholics. For a moment it felt like we were both there, watching King Henry's principal apologist and prayer-changer suffer his turn at the stake, thanks and no thanks to Bloody Mary's body burners this time. We both had a few moments of silence, me at least trying to visualise the religious cruelties of Tudor times. Then came the thunderclap. Dr. Kenny just as quietly went on:

"That is where Paisley stands when he comes to Oxford, to preach at us. Whatever else you do about Ireland, it is Paisley you will have to deal with in the end".

Here I am at the apex of English political intellect and listening to this Oxford Fellow talking rubbish. Paisley!—the rabble rouser intent on wrecking the Presbyterian Church in Ireland while he grabbed their malcontents for his own bucket-collection chapels—a dauber of walls and a wrecker of shops showing Irish goods, a neo Fascist parading on a mountain top with followers waving their gun licences. Such advice, from that source, in 1985, made public, would have been widely derided. How could this Thomist Don, or anyone else, have foretold that the roaring Pauline preacher, (He has earned measurable credit for his essays on St.Paul), would have his own Damascus moment for Catholics more than twenty years later. The "Mad Doctor" that poor little Brian Faulkner accused of pulling down the last three Stormont's prime ministers, him, Chichester Clark and "O'Neill of the Nuns", continued toppling everyone else's pulpits and prams for another twenty years and more. And yet, this is my own guess, the conversion that led him to share power with the deputy commander of the IRA—"the Chuckle Brothers" episode—was by Rome, not the papacy as such, but the city crowded by most of the world leaders paying their last respects to the most charismatic pope of centuries. John Paul the iron-curtain breaking Pole died in the summer of 2005. Ian Paisley was near to death at that time in an illness we know nothing of, still, and then struggling back to life.

Did he wonder, watching the Rome funeral on television,—who would follow his cortege? Did he make a Pauline vow? We mere mortals may never know.

Emerging again, he signalled his conversion with a calm, smiling visit to a Catholic primary school in his Bannside constituency. He airily waved away the commotion it caused—sure didn't he do this all the time. Not since an image of Jesus throwing Saul from his horse had such a change round occurred (No nuns with buns for tea this time, Ireland has almost run out of them, and it shows.)

Northern Ireland's mandatory D'Hondt-style coalition, imported from Belgium, where as with the first assembly formed by the Belfast Agreement, it has failed again. It is seen to be fragile if nothing else. Its main weakness, openly acknowledged, is its dependence on the chalk and cheese leadership confined to Sinn Fein and the DUP, denying shared leadership to the three other parties. Its more serious long-term weakness, to be rumbled sooner than later, is the reduced franchise of the Unionist majority, their voting about as useless as that of the Irish Nationalists during the fifty-year Stormont junta of 1922-1972. Irrespective of how they vote they must share power with their deadliest enemies openly proclaiming their target around or soon after 2016 for the demise of the state in the centenary of the Easter Rising. And the Catholics, they are again locked into second place; nothing has changed but the shape of the place.

The only way out is a shared parliamentary capital of all Ireland on a neutral site. It works in so many other places redolent of the same historical foundations. It is impossible to imagine Canada without the calming restraints of Ottawa, without which French Catholic Montreal and British Protestant (Orange Order-led) Toronto would resemble polarised Dublin and Belfast for much the same two centuries.

The legislation, written by the same civil service policy wonks who had written Versailles, and then probably Locarno, is in the 1920 Better Government of Ireland Act. The clause allowing both Irish parliaments to sit anywhere they please was copied by DeValera into the 1937 Constitution, Bunreacht na hEireann, for the Dail. The Trust's single-sheet A4 policy papers managed to get the Irish Cabinet moving around the country, their compromise to our request to move the Dail for a day or two, as a first step. I had returned to Ireland, to live in my native Armagh in 1994, at the request of several trustees who insisted the Trust would work better in Ireland than from England. I came alone; by then all my children were doing what they wanted to do. In a sequence I can't quite remember without ransacking my files, I was interviewed at length in Armagh by Peter Smith of the Northern Ireland Office, latterly promoted to the UK Embassy in Washington, and an advisor to Taoiseach John Bruton in Government

Buildings, Dublin. The first result in the south was, rather than move the Dail, and anyway having gone out of office unexpectedly in 1997, John Bruton took his Fine Gael shadow cabinet to Limerick, a welcome response to the city corporation which voted unanimously the year before to invite the Dail to sit there in honour of their unbroken eight centuries of civic rule since King John gave it to them in the 12th century. Whereupon, the incoming Taoiseach Bertie Ahern informed the Trust that this policy of moving the cabinet around would continue, Mr. Ahern also advised me, a different letter, that to move the Dail I would have to ask the Oireachtas via the Ceann Comhairle—the Speaker to English readers. In a third letter, May 29 2001, responding to two of mine ("Dear Paddy")—the Taoiseach stoutly defended Dublin's history as capital, never really a reality outside the 122 years of union. Like the tale of America being formed by English Protestant dissidents, Dublin's stand as traditional capital of Ireland is mere role playing. Mr. Ahern conceded that the sharing of a capital's functions, *"if not the location, might arise for discussion, if in the future the two parts of Ireland come to decide that they wanted to come together."* This was the first time I have experienced any Irish leader describing unity in that mutual way, but his letter contained a common error on the neutral capital which many statesmen and others share. It is not the icing on the cake of any kind of political agreement or treaty, it is the cake, the solution all on its own which dissolved most other problems. Either way, none of these developments beyond and after the Limerick invitation, ever saw the light of day in the Irish Times, Ireland's self-described "paper of record" and that was not my fault.

The first move from the North;—the Executive got into their Ford Mondeos and drove to Armagh to meet the Irish Cabinet (all lined up in their Mercs across the lane to the CoI archbishops's former palace) together, in one room, across one long table. I felt I was just moving in events. I did not feel that I had "made" Irish history, that came later. The Northern Ireland office acknowledged my role as a guest but had no room for me in the palace room and shifted me to the press tent, wherefrom I delivered a speech of welcome, unaware I was being broadcast by the BBC. No ringing phrases have stayed in my memory, but proud of myself as I spoke like my father, without notes, off the cuff. My audience was composed largely of the international press, about 100 people. I know I made an impression. First Minister David Trimble, early in my opening sentences, turned suddenly to the Deputy First Minister, Seamus Mallon, as I lip-read him, saying: "Dig the bow tie Seamus, getta load of the bow tie."

So there was some harmony between them, unlike the day I told Armagh business promoters way back in the 'Seventies, trying to launch a cider industry, to forget the apples and just bottle the water. Nineteen years later, Ireland brimming with sixteen water-bottling companies grossing I was told, £100m in product and labour, all based on my opening memo to the Response from Industry Foundation, a business promotion agency formed in response to Jack Lynch's election victory in 1977. I learned that four closely concerned people had tried to have me certified to St. Luke's Psychiatric Hospital, Armagh. I by-passed St. Luke's but only by the fluke of Harold Wilson's Order in Council to make such moves possible only by two independent doctors. The Irish Times, the self annointed 'Ireland's Paper of Record' treats me as if I was there ever since.

* * *

CHAPTER SIXTEEN

Averill Lukic Intervenes

In 1971, when the Nigerian Civil War ended, two million dead, my adopted step-daughter Averill (McGarvey) Lukic, was betimes an assistant editor of the London-based shipping and economics newspaper, West Africa, following that as foundation-editor of Nigeria Newsletter, both under the patronage of the Daily Mirror, owners of a newspaper group in Nigeria.

Her interest in Africa stemmed from her A-Level French, marked "off the card" as exceptional, added to the luck of an early boyfriend introducing her to The Observer's Africa specialist, Colin Legum. He was about to commence forming his reference book, Africa Who's Who, and needed an assistant, fluent French speaker. It was her first job.

Averill called me at the Sunday Telegraph to tell me Nigeria's media offices were re-opening their London bureaux, and many were anxious to cover the "British Civil War." I was about to crib that that one had ended three centuries ago when the penny dropped that it was my poor bloody Ulster they meant, which is not in Britain. Would I brief them for her, she asked, and so I did, in several offices between Fleet Street and High Holborn. When we reached the "no solution" hiatus that was bothering everybody, then and since, I airily dismissed this with the outline of a neutral shared capital for North and South. It could be an Irish version of neutral capitals throughout several former empires of old Europe. I cited Washington DC, begun late in the 18th century, Ottawa in the 19th century, and Canberra as the 20th century began. A shade over 20 years later, the 20th century ending, Nigeria announced that her new neutral capital, not Christian Lagos, not Moslem Kano, but Abuja "was open for business."

The news did not catch the attention that it deserved. The announcement, in 1992, clashed with the worldwide horror at the "ethnic cleansing" that had broken out in the fracturing provinces of Yugoslavia that were to become separate countries. But Nigeria began to grow up. The new capital brought ethnic peace across many tribes and dialects. Economic rebels still struggle in the oilfields against exploitation, and there have been recent bursts of religious fighting in the neighbourhoods of the new capital. Nevertheless Nigeria is visibly maturing. Did my recall of an old idea from other ex-colonies, provide the solution? Of course it did, just as the first domino knocks down the last one. Ms Averill McGarvey Lukic tipped over the first one, me, her adoptive step-father, the last one.

The conception and building of Abuja—Venerated Rock, every country has such a place—was hastened by the relentless congestion that was choking Lagos, a problem still widening, or rather lengthening in Ireland, the Belfast-Dublin corridor's creeping development along the east coast. Across Ireland, across the Shannon to the west, virtually everywhere is facing decline and even decay. A shared New Tara in the Boyne Valley, historically romantic, and of political origin to both states, would nevertheless serve the need less than say, Ballyjamesduff, County Cavan.

OK, OK!—Yes, I know it's that place in Percy French's song inviting Paddy Reilly to come home, but that is no reason to dismiss its geo-position in the Republic's part of Ulster, and so close to the border. The location, surrounded by scenic lakes and indifferent pasture, thus ideal to build on, resembles the choice the Australians took for Canberra in 1901, placing it in the larger state, New South Wales, but close to the border with smaller Victoria. Just as important, a shared parliamentary capital at Ballyjamesduff provides a form of unification in a part of Ulster the northern unionists originally wanted, but abandoned for fear of being out-voted. They have no such fear now, a recent poll in Northern Ireland revealed a majority of Catholics, ergo Nationalists, in favour of remaining in the union. (Quite a few of them might have been Poles) What harm is there in a Union Jack bird when the nest is indisputably Irish anyway, north or south, and so, better the devil you know. I have suspected that reasoning was in some degree present in the North long before I stood for Labour in Mid-Ulster. As for now, in a changing Ireland, would Co. Cavan concede a Danzig corridor to Northern Ireland? Just ask.

With or without a shared capital—as clearly hinted in the 1920 Better Government of Ireland Act—watch out now as we approach the fore and after of their centenary, for the development of real ideological political parties in both Irish states. The neutral capital, sharing two much smaller parliaments as well, possibly even shared ministries, will hasten the arrival of new politics, as well as arresting the decline of the west and north-west. The untrammelled recognition of each by the other will dilute partition well beyond the near insignificant role it has today. The conditional recognition in the failed Good Friday Agreement and its four patchwork renewals must be overtaken, the limited franchise of the unionists, must be replaced with a vote of open results.

Political change is hard to come by in Ireland, in the South especially, where new parties rise and then fade into the old civil war argument In January 2005, mid-way in the Assembly's five years of silence, which was predicted by the Trust to the British Irish Inter Parliamentary Body in March 2002, we showed the Assembly could sustain itself with a fixed five-year term, impervious to the "one out, all out" trigger" of automatic dissolution it still retains.

The two First Minister positions should be rotated around all five participating parties, for durations proportionate to their size, say from six months to eighteen months. In 2005 the Trust published these and some easier links in a full page advertisement in both Irish editions of the Daily Mirror., January 6, Epiphany, day of renewal. It was ignored by the serried ranks of Irish media, verbally and vocally, institutionally uptight against any form of novelty from non official sources. The Daily Mirror trousered our £3000 while omitting the ad from the Republic edition. After my fulminating protest it appeared there on the 7th January. Rescued yet again by the whim of a chuckling brother, it is still a stratified assembly in a hall of mirrors.

Conor Brady, who was editor of the Irish Times over the latter period of "the armed struggle" wrote in his former paper that the North's bloody tumult had matured national Irish journalism out of a narrow introspection. Well, up to a point, Lord Conor—after all, if bombs are going off in the street and off-duty cops are being shot dead on their own doorsteps, often in full view of their children (the cruellest of all said Cardinal Cahal Daly) you can't hold the front page until the relevant minister says something. The paper is one of the best broadsheets in these islands, especially in the pages of its arts reviewing and sport. The paper more often resembles Little Jack Horner, still sat in that corner, publishing its own curds and whey; any suggestion from anywhere that the Dail should be moved well away from Dublin is an unprintable heresy. Criticism of the ruling apparatus in Belfast as such, is seen as unbecoming behaviour to a neighbour; let sleeping dogs lie. Oh, and Conor, that was a very expensive medicine it took for you garsuns and ladies to bestir yourselves out of dreamland. The self-annointed journal of Irish record can often detail on Tuesday morning the reasons for a riot in Manchuria on Monday, thanks to an expatriate journalist living in the region, thus free from the confines and rules of any old Tara Street testament. The Irish Times is an open haven for aspiring university fellows to have their theories or research items illuminated over a signature that identifies writer and university. No lesser fry need bother. Others, like me, from the pre-Kinnock generation in Britain—too poor for university—must avail themselves of the letters page if wishing to announce something new. About a decade after receiving that instruction by letter from a page editor, it was endorsed again by "Madam" Geraldine Kennedy, one of her friendlier rebuffs. I warmly congratulated her when she became the first woman editor, regretting that I did not add the warning that the most talented reporters, and she was certainly that, do not necessarily make good editors. As far as I was concerned, a thrice returned expatriate, an innovative unsalaried innovator, a story maker, Kennedy, as far as my constructive work was concerned, might just as well been one of the women knitting at a blunt guillotine. The some-things "new" I have always proposed on behalf of the researching Trust have working precedents in the Commonwealth and outside, while others lie buried, unread by Irish journalists and university historians, in the 1920 Act. The 1922 Treaty, extolled for its 90th anniversary in 2012, was merely a working relationship document. Has anyone any advance on roughly 25 rejections over 20 years? The Irish Independent and the (now) Irish Examiner, have both published constitution-framing articles by me; the two Belfast morning papers, The Newsletter and the Irish News, have not only published me, they have done so simultaneously, each cross-referencing the other. They did so several times, on my direct pleas to them, ending nearly a century of pointless animosity as their readers burned. (The Irish News was founded in the wake of Parnell's *mesalliance* with the frisky hankie dropper, Mrs. Kitty O'Shea, to spur his political end; he was washed out anyway long before; The Newsletter is roughly a century older). The editors won prizes and international recognition. Did they mention me, or Irish Parliament Trust? I'll give you one guess. Go on! It's easy. The answer has only two letters.

The D'Hondt Rule by which Northern Ireland is framed in a politically neutered parliament, insists that all parties with membership of two or more, must participate in the cabinet of government. It has (fractured) working precedent in Belgium. "Plucky little Belgium" as the Brits patronise her, divided by language and race and held together under "the King of the Belgians" has imploded into nearly a dozen mini-states with their own parliaments and assemblies. To favour D'Hondt success, but more likely an attempt to widen tolerance, German has been admitted as an official language, and some of the states want diplomatic representation overseas. Got that!

In 2007, the year Belfast was moving towards another try at ruling the province under these imported strictures, the Belgian Government collapsed, was ruled for a while since by an agreed committee, was still without government after an election in 2010, then managed to get a cabinet together just before Christmas 2011. Northern Ireland struggles on in the 2012 leadership of bored ministers and parties uncertain of their future, "hanging on for now to nurse, for fear of finding something worse." as Chesterton puts it (Oh, a Catholic, sorry).

This irony is sharpened by the certain knowledge that nothing remotely like it could be sustained in the South. Hang on a minute, there is a comparison. Imperialists in coalition with Republicans in the North, enforced, are not far removed from the right with left in the coalitions that Dublin, in sheer desperation frequently cobbles up. In 2009, serious dissension to Dail misjudgements became apparent in the angry streets of the South's capital. Either side, whatever coalition, will always try to make the poor pay for the malfunctions and greed of the rich. Bankers default, hiding each other's loans, so medical card holders were asked to surrender their rights. The aged of Ireland took to the streets. Behind everything else in the day to day "fluff" in the media lies the fear that Article Fifteen of the constitution might be used to move the government permanently away from Dublin. The licence to do so was copied (from the Westminster Act) into the 1937 Bunreacht na hEireann by its main progenitor, Eamon DeValera

In that ignored Mirror advert, the Trust also reminded the protagonists of the biggest miss of all, bigger in its end result, and yet easier to try. This was the 1920 Act's licence for ministers of state in both Houses to sit and debate in the other one, but not vote. It is painful to try and imagine the saner history we might have had if only that clause was used. It now brings gasps of astonishment from politicians of all ages, the public even more so, whenever the Trust has broached it.

Then think of what we have now, across two states struggling for self-finance, or from somewhere, someone, anywhere, willing to cough up the cash. But let us consider those other shams, the Cross Border

Authorities with Executive Power, six to start with, expanding to 12 in due course. (Perhaps the Twelve have arrived; you would never know) They have the executive power of a bumble bee in a rookery, and perhaps better named as Share Exchanges. Each must consult their two parent ministers. The result is that the five million or so Irelanders I think we have about now—if we have that many left, now have 37 departments of state nearly a third of them pointless. As political window dressing, they are far from cost endurable. This paragraph was first written in early 2008, the year of the Bursting Bubble. I no more than many people who should have, did not foresee the economic collapse, but I was increasingly nervous of the soaring cost of housing, on the verge several times of writing a critical warning letter to the Irish Times as the most visible coachman flogging the housing horses, and enjoying the resulting profits from advertising.

The Trust's research and publications veered away from the obviously romantic view that the Boyne Valley was the site for a shared capital. Still regarding it as the key to future peaceful and co-operative links between North and South, we came up with Ballyjamesduff as a place and name for a better geographical link. The economic plight of both Irelands in the global mish-mash now reinforce that choice. A new parliament city in the north-north-west will create new money and stimulate industries from the cottage variety upward, the very sort hailed on the morning I am writing this in January 2012 by a leader in the Irish Times (Hurrah!). There is an example of this in the neighbouring island. When the Queen's children and in-laws started moving westward to villas and old mansions in the western Cotswolds, many of the (t) wee townships from the Chilterns westward were re-invigorated by the arts as well as many of the wider cottage industries. R&D on special innovations opened up all over. Even Bristol University rose in several measures from western somnolence to a noticeable intellectual niche. No doubt a few court jesters moved west as well.

OK, readers are screaming about the cost. Fear not, the solution to that is simple, as the meerkats so wisely say in those insurance ads. Rule out the huge and reckless capital projects to ease the strains of Dublin's over-growth. Baile atha Cliath will remain an important civic and social centre, but will not need new railways, a tunnel under the Liffey, or acres of more housing estates. Abandon that stupid idea of syphoning the river Shannon into Dublin's bathrooms.

The last line I read on the development of the Luas tram system, a good idea, included the teeth-cracking E62m—a-kilometre it was going to cost linking the dock developments with bendy trams. Is it not time for

Ireland to build its first parliament fit for purpose, and for the visitors from over the way. Partition has never in my Armagh childhood and wartime tea smuggling experience been anything like a European frontier. Even if partition remains on the statute book, it will have ebbed away by osmosis, if only we can aspire to enjoy what we have, and let a more soothing future take good care of the peace.

The former Irish Guards officer who led us in the North for a while, who must have, as others of his rank taking the British Army's "Buggins Turn", marched a share of the battalion to Sunday Mass, *so like having tea with Reverend Mother, the headmistress of a Catholic school, was no big deal for this Protestant Prime Minister.* Terence O'Neill, who pushed me towards the Northern Ireland Secretary of State, James Prior, as being more important to me than he was, may be resting at ease in his grave now in the belief, like mine, that the Paisley vendetta that had him flung from office for that crime, is no more. We have a New Ireland, if still drifting. It needs work. It lacks new thinking. It is to this O'Neill that we owe amends.

CHAPTER SEVENTEEN

Just Some More Bits

The Irish Examiner, then called The Cork Examiner, was the only one of the four morning papers in the Irish Republic to publish this article on February 1, 1993.

"This could well be the year of the Irish Solution to the Irish Question. On the day I penned that line, Cardinal Cahal Daly was saying much the same thing."

A few weeks before, on January 6 (Epiphany, the 12th Day of Christmas, a day of renewal in Christian countries) the Catholic nationalist daily in Belfast, The Irish News, and its Protestant unionist rival, The Newsletter, published the same article from the director of Irish Parliament Trust. **The article continued**;

For all of this century both papers have either ignored each other or fought prolonged bouts of bitter political and religious quarrelling. Yet, on this unique occasion, the editors independently saw the article as showing the way forward to their deeply polarised readers. As its author, in my capacity as director of the Trust, I then persuaded both Belfast editors to print on the same day.

In short, the same political-constitutional plan had crossed the peace line. By a wonderful coincidence, the day chosen by mutual space and paging reasons was Wednesday January 6th—Epiphany. There must be an added message there for all of us.

Here is the key to it. Virtually every country overseas that was ruled by a former imperial power, Britain, France, Russia, Spain, Portugal, Turkey, has rejected the former imperial capital in favour of somewhere neutral. The idea is based on one central theme—the desire of the former colonists to rid themselves of the tyranny of European-style religious-city states, which many of them had fled.

The essence of our quarrel is that we have two of them, our ethnic capitals of Belfast and Dublin, neither of which is acceptable to large sections of the Irish population. The American rebels began it with their refusal to accept Protestant Boston (as it was in 1780) or Quaker Philadelphia, and so, they chose a virgin site, an Indian settlement called Potowmack.

Canada, almost by accident, followed suit, but unlike the Americans changing its name to honour Washington, they retained the Indian name, Ottawa. So did the Australians; Canberra is Aboriginal for "meeting place". And so did the Nigerians. Abuja, only 13 months a capital, means Central Rock.

Ireland has its own Canberra, and if we moved to it we could see an end to the sectarian bitterness, because that's what Canberra did for Australia. It's called Tara, abutting the Boyne Valley, an area of our national life and history that encompasses the origins of everything that we are.

Preferably, the site for a neutral capital, in Ireland's case to be mutually shared, should be "aboriginal" and virginal, but some countries choose a mutual city for their third place. Just over a year ago the Soviet Union turned itself into the Commonwealth of Independent States, with a neutral capital, which, reported TIME magazine, "was not in Red Moscow, not in Czarist St. Petersburg, but in Plain Jane Minsk." Historically, the Americans knew the score, and what was afoot.

So the lesson here is, not in Belfast, not in Dublin, but . . . .

Rooted deeply to our Irish division is the thought that Stormont is in Belfast for evermore and the Dail is in Dublin for all eternity. That idea is misconceived.

The 1920 Government of Ireland Act (full name The **Better** Government of Ireland Act) says that both Irish parliaments can move anywhere they chose. Bunreacht na hEireann 1937, (the newer constitution introduced by Eamon DeValera) placing the Dail in or near Dublin, adds in Clause 15, "or in such other place as they may from time to time determine."

I would dearly like to see the Dail come to Cork for a day or two to show willingness for the change we must have (Just imagine the startling change in their outlook that would bring us!)

Eighteen months ago I showed our Irish plans to the EC conference on Yugoslavia. Both negotiators accepted it, Lord Carrington especially, remembering his time as High Commissioner to Canberra.

On Sunday January 14th, as I am writing this, radio and TV are referring to Sarajevo's future as "the neutral capital" of Bosnia. Like the Cardinal, I, too, have high hopes that 1993 is the year of the Irish solution.

(End of *Cork Examiner article*)

* * *

Well, it was not. (But in June 2005, twelve years later, the Irish Government sat for a day in Cork, amid great jubilation) But I was wrong claiming Canada had followed Washington DC. She did, but the Swiss, when imperial France was forced to leave in 1848, beat them to it naming tiny Berne as their neutral capital to the model neutral state of several languages, races and religions, beat them to second place.

A footnote to the 1993 Examiner article described the Trust as a registered British charity and the only independent research foundation working on Ireland's British problem, with trustees in Ireland, Britain and America. So the research went on. In the decade that followed, the romantic notion of a shared new Tara in the Boyne Valley ruled itself out for the realism that Dublin had almost grown out to it. Every morning, returning every evening, columns of single-occupant cars just grew and grew, like Topsy on a roll, fifty to seventy miles north, west and south. By the end of the nineties the "queue" to get into Dublin from the northern counties alone ran back to Kells, and then, Cavan, a crawling circus for nearly seventy miles. What to do to fix this? More tunnels and railway lines for the big city of course. A new trams system was built and like all other capital projects in Ireland the cost outran by mega-thousands the original estimate and the financial practicality of the idea. Never mind, we'll tap the Shannon with a great big pipe to bring more drinking water to Dublin as it grows and grows. Because of an intended friendship bond, betrothal, or even a marriage with Northern Ireland, a shared capital has to be further north. For the sake of western Ireland and the need to sustain its populations against decay and migration (now visible again) it also had to have a demographic pull that stretched to the Atlantic coast, which ruled out the east coast.

First thought: Place it in one of the Ulster counties not in Northern Ireland

Second Thought: The Ulster plantation in volume terms stopped at County Cavan because the land is so poor, so place it there.

Third Thought. Ballyjamesduff for a host of reasons. (Ireland's Bern?) Also legendary in song at least (*Come back Paddy Riley to Ballyjamesduff* in the memorable lyrics of Percy French) the handsome little town has a name you cannot forget, beginning with the Viking "bailie", ergo bailiwick, fenced off area, small town, and at some stage it was expanded or perhaps owned by a Scots-Irishman called James Duff. Another simple translation to Middle Irish will tell you it's the Place of Dark Seamus. County Cavan is replete with wonderful lake-lands, and at its centre a magnificent town square with an amenable people who would just love the idea. Way back in the 'Sixties I had to ring a local solicitor on a four-hour delay between Dublin and the town, a common handicap at the time. I booked the call to Ballyjamesduff One. The operator, four hours later, got me Ballyjamesduff Two.

I groaned at the thought of another four-hour wait, but "Two" asked me who I wanted and I told him. He roared "He's standing in the middle of the square talking to the town clerk at this moment, hold on there now and I'll get him for you", and he did. Greater courtesy I have never known on a phone call. Its location, for both parts of Ireland, equidistant from Dublin and Belfast, closely resembles Canberra's for Australia. Built in the last century on the fringe of New South Wales and close to loyal Victoria, by an American architect, Walter Burley Griffin, and master-minded by a politican of Mayo parents, King O'Malley, facts I thought I might just mention here, in the reign of a Mayo Taoiseach in Dublin. The Mayo County Council, Enda, keep an archive on King O'Malley—as my research Trust discovered in Australia. About twelve years ago I was saying that Peter Robinson would be the best Taoiseach we'll never have, but you never know.

The choice and go-ahead for Ottawa to play the same role for Canada in the 19th century was down to another Irishman, James D'Arcy McGee, poet, Fenian statesman, and brilliant orator, for which reason, as Canada's children are told in class, his is the second name on Canada's Foundation Roll of Honour.

I wrote most of these paragraphs on a day the TV news showed a Dublin newsboy holding aloft an Evening Herald front page starkly proclaiming BLACK THURSDAY. (September 30th 2010) so of course we will be told we could not possibly afford a new capital in these years of extreme fiscal failure and four years straitened partial recovery. But the refrain—we cannot afford it—is spurious. New capitals, as per the poorest country Bangladesh, create new money. They also create new endeavour in related fields. (Trade follows the Flag). In 2009, trying to get Dail Eireann to observe Clause 15 and move ceremoniously for a day in honour of Kilkenny city this time, and its four centuries of borough status from King James 1st (the town is much older than that) I was sharply rebuffed by the Ceann Comhairle Mr. John O'Donoghue TD, while Ireland's oldest civic city got a rejection by return of post from his office neighbour in Government Buildings, then the Clerk of the Dail and Secretary General, Mr. Kieran Coughlan. We could not afford it. Way back in 1996, the then Clerk of the Dail frightened Limerick Corporation off their unanimous invitation to the Dail in honour of their octocentenary of King John's civic foundation, with more than twenty unquantified cost items which included that of moving RTE's broadcasting apparatus to Limerick, and the provision of voting rooms. Mr. Coughlan sent me a copy of his warning list to Limerick. Irish Parliament Trust had never suggested, and neither had the city fathers, that the Dail should legislate on such occasions. As for the expense, as many TDs would have had shorter trips to parliament as those having longer journeys. Mind you, that thought was offered before we realised the gargantuan texture of parliamentary expenses in Leinster House as well as Westminster.

And yet, a surprise for all, Kerry's Big John was sensitive to anyone being grandiose with travel plans, before he himself became one of the grandest on the roads to anywhere the two government jobs in turn took him.

Newly invited as Official Observer to the British Irish Inter Parliamentary Body (which is a Leinster House-Westminster copycat of the Trust's role for the Dail and Stormont, except they had salaries and state money) I began my nine-year attendance, sans fees or expenses, at Adare Castle, Limerick in 1996. Explaining my work and ideas in a coffee break that for instance the Dail could actually sit in Armagh for a day, the tall, smartly-tailored backbencher O'Donoghue disengaged himself with ease from his coffee circle, and leaned over into my coffee circle with the retort: "The Dail in Armagh! By God we'll send you the Travellers."

There was a united roar of laughter from the members of Leinster House and the Commons. It subsided quicker than a duck in a moat-house, so sudden was the realisation they were being a bit off-colour. Three years later, in December 1999, a full Irish Cabinet sat facing the full Northern Irish Executive in one room across one table in my beautiful birthplace of Armagh. The Irish Minister for Justice, Mr. John O'Donoghue, TD, all the way from Kerry, was very visibly present. The Travellers were not represented. But I was there, as the originator of the idea, though not the location, thanks to John Bruton's compromise in taking his shadow cabinet to Limerick in 1997. This country-changing moment was taken up very quickly by incoming Taoiseach Bertie Ahern, in not one but three letters to me, for the cabinet. The two Irish ruling cabinets got on very well, then and since. Sauce for the cabinet geese, is surely sauce for the parliamentary ganders. Stand aside Baile atha Cliath and Bel Feiste, Cead Mile Failte Baile Seamus Dubh.

* * *

EPILOGUE

Remember the story and picture by the war-photographer in Vietnam who was confronted by a little girl, only eight or nine years old, starkly visible in a total nakedness that would shock the world? She was running away from American napalm bombing, delivered by Vietnamese pilots in American planes. A glancing fireball had stripped her. It was the war's most memorable picture, as he instinctively knew, but then thinking more of his civilised manhood than his photography, he ran after the terrified child and covered her with his own coat. A few years ago, one of the happier hinges of fate, he took pictures at her wedding in America. Vietnam was an American series of mistakes, as on that occasion equipping South Vietnam pilots with napalm bombs. Well, here's another one stepping outside the professional frame. What is the point of reporting a war if you can see clearly the best way to end it, and abolish its causes. Not that I was doing such reporting. The Sunday Telegraph sent me home to write on it just the once. The most memorable incident for me took place in Belfast at the Duke of York bar, a haunt of journalists. A favoured, readable columnist on The Newsletter (with a proud tag as the world's oldest daily newspaper) Ralph "Bud" Bossence, suddenly reached over the bar and grabbed a bent and hungry looking youth in a potboy's brown work-coat: "Here Gerry, you talk to Paddy here, a big fireman from London. Paddy, you watch this boy, he's going places." Bud died youngish, too young to see where Gerry was going. When President Mary Robinson shook hands with Adams to an outcry of anger, she created a political issue for over a year. I was away ahead of the game, since abandoning the nationalism of my father to fight Mid Ulster for union-supporting Labour. When the Secretary of State, Michael Ancram, eventually did, he was interrupting a chat with me. The Belfast Telegraph photo shows a grinning Martin McGuinness stretching out his hand too. Then or now, I would have followed the naked

Vietnam girl with my coat, but I could never have shaken Adams's hand a second time. He has too much to explain. In 1985, I had already shaken a political hand with Senator Robinson, long before anybody else had, in this context, recognising her potential in leadership. She had the courage to denounce the Anglo Irish Agreement as "punitive" to the Unionists, earning a dismissal from the bone-headed Labour leadership, four years before they suddenly recognised her potential as a candidate for the Presidency. Alas, Mary did not see mine. We sat uncomfortably on a broken sofa in the Dail tea-toom, nursing teacups on saucers while she gently rubbished my outline of a parliamentary capital for Ireland, the solution that would bring a solution.

In 1994, by which time Robinson had been selected in 1990, elected and had served most of a term as a ground-breaking President, I went back to Ireland for the third time, I gave Ireland more than my coat, spending most of the equity profit on three houses in succession to support my family and then myself. After eight years the trustees of the charity I had wanted her to lead, and unable to find her match, decided I could run it myself, and better from my native island. I went home to Armagh, on my own, the children up and away and all for the most part doing what they wanted to do. I stumbled into the unpublished papers of a dead Protestant Primate of all Ireland who urged his fellow Unionist confreres to erect Ulster's devolved parliament in Armagh.

"It is the more ameliorating place for a parliament for everybody". Dr. Charles D'Arcy's idea at Armagh (1920-28) had been totally forgotten. In a lengthening lifetime I had never heard or read a word of this idea. He was eventually talked out of it by a delegation of Unionist leaders, Lord Bangor among them. Pointing a peer at an Archbishop was the thing, especially one owning an estate on the fringes of east Belfast called Stormont. The Archbishop was so put down about the idea he did not mentioned it in either of the two books of memoirs he wrote.

So I simply proposed the erection of a Peace Pavilion for the divided country, and any others needing a cheaper quieter English-speaking Geneva for peace parleys. The local churches could use it too. I also correctly estimated, in the Commission's request on maintenance of such a building, that whatever its role, the British and Irish governments would share all or most of it. I argued with myself and some others, as director of Irish Parliament Trust. The British government had just set up the Millennium Commission, furnished with shed-loads of cash to seek out pioneering effort of exceptional quality to mark ten centuries past with something to observe the next ten. In particular, they wanted to see new buildings for fresh purpose. The Commission thought the Trust was a trifle detached from bricks and mortar and asked me for partners. The City Council had to be my first choice, and they readily agreed. On innovation of this kind they were guided by a brilliant Town Clerk, Des Mitchell, who was recognised for his balanced drive with a council enduring the standard Northern Irish division earmarked by religious division coinciding with the defence or denial of the state itself. His successor, John Briggs, generously volunteered to this writer "He was by far the best Town Clerk Armagh has ever had."

Queen's University Outreach was the other likely partner then conducting a day-student system in the City for people of all ages and missed chances. The very beautiful main building of the County Infirmary had been altered inside and restored around it. Its director, Gary Sloan asked me to seek the University's consent, and so I wrote to the Pro Vice Chancellor, inviting the university to be my partner. The PVC was a Dr. Mary McAleese. She gave the go ahead and joined me with the added suggestion the Pavilion should be used to solve religious conflict. When my first Mary-President-to be eventually indicated she might not serve out the full seven-year term, my second "Mary-President-to-be, indicated she would relinquish Queen's, where she was the second woman to hold the job, and first Catholic, and successfully run for that office. You see, believe this or not; on this remarkable journey of mine. I keep getting signals, in the midst of a chorus of concern and denial from the closest of friends, most of them fretting about my mental welfare, that I am, was, on the right track to achieve peace in Ireland. The signals come earthbound but often felt heaven-led, even associations with the name Mary. I lean heavily along this difficult path on the Mother of God, even though just mentioning her views had me thrown out of the Sovereign Affairs Committee of the British Irish Inter Parliamentary Body during its plenary session in Kilkenny. This was to be a sampler to the main body, the invitation was the first to an unelected outsider of the Body, which followed my research charity into existence and copying its purpose for London and Dublin. I got as far as saying that the least likely fan of the Good Friday Agreement had to be the Blessed Virgin herself. The British side of the table erupted in a series of coughs and double humphing, the Irish side just coughing with bowed heads. It was no good. I faintly recall being told they would be "in touch". Six months later in England's Hanbury Manor Hotel, Ware (a former convent) they gave my promised speaking slot to Professor Paul Bew, another Queens' star, who told them that unless the IRA (an illicit organisation) came in and signed on the dotted line, alongside Sinn Fein (a duality of IRA membership) there would be no home rule, no assembly. I had wanted to tell them to ignore the IRA pull, and put the new assembly somewhere else, just as Dr. D'Arcy tried.

The British co-chairman MP, David Winnick, told me bluntly I was too eccentric to address the Body. Seconds later I confronted Bew in conversation with Mr. Kevin McNamara, MP; did he really think the IRA must be in Government, and he confirmed the line from his speech. Mr. McNamara sped away in high good humour. The Hansard report at Ware of the Kilkenny meeting included this summary by Mr. Jim O'Keefe, co-chairman of the Sovereign Matters Group:

In Kilkenny, we had an interesting and impressive presentation of the views of Paddy McGarvey of the Irish Parliament Trust. Many of you will be aware of those, and he has again kept us up to date by circulating his latest memo at this meeting. We appreciate the opportunity to listen to him and thank him for his presentation.

How nice, especially for the Body's only speaking outsider, but only after they stopped me speaking and politely showed me the door. The IRA and Paisley's DUP sharing the top roles in government, the essence of the Bew speech, is tolerable to British and Irish parliamentarians. My plan for a neutral site parliamentary centre for two freely-franchised parliaments, an Irish version of the Commonwealth's most successful peace system, too "eccentric" for them?

But back to Armagh and the Millennium Commission, All three partners survived three stages before a curious rejection with the advice to do more work, and return with details of a building and finance. That ruled me and the Trust out. Charity rules in Britain frowned on incurring debts. I left the whole caboodle with the Council and the University Outreach (which has since abandoned its interest and presence in Armagh). In February 2010, long since back in England, I learned to my astonishment (although 16 years is only a short time in constitutional politics) it was nearing completion as a parliament chamber for the two Irish cabinets, sitting as the North South Ministerial Council. It is a compromise first step to the Trust's 25-year campaign that the solution for Ireland is a shared parliamentary capital, and which, I insist to the derision of former colleagues, has to be the solution for Israel-Palestine as well, or something very like it. (Well, think about it, for both of us). In all the information I have obtained since, the now retired

Town Clerk and chief executive of the city and district council, Des Mitchell, is the man who carried it forward. The day I gave him the drawings of the concept laid out in Sherry's Field, made by my landscape-architect son Feargus as a gift to the Trust, he said: "I want to see that building in Armagh." And so there it is, except that the site was changed by a few hundred yards to that of the beloved City Hall, burned down by Republican rioters in 1970. This was another "signal" for me—and an emotional moment for my sister Nuala—this Pax Hibernia building replaced the one where my father worked nearly all his life as senior clerk to the Lavery family of solicitors, (son, Hugh, a Recorder Judge in Belfast, Cecil, President of the Supreme Court) not to mention his other office, same building of course, during his many random years as city councillor, and its frequent chairman. Some will think my head is as big as is clearly evident, others will understand; I felt that all of this, all the way back to the Nigerian journalists I was briefing for Averill in 1971, was a job I was meant to do.

CONSIDER IRELAND TODAY, and then think Israel-Palestine.
A 19th century Irish song wails *"It's the most distressing country that ever yet was seen"* Under the boot of angry English coercion acts, the singer complains "They're hanging men and women for the wearin' of the Green."—a touch of poetic license in the land of Saints and Scholars.

The plight of Northern Ireland is not their fault either. A mandatory coalition which devalues the franchise of Protestant unionists, as previously applied by them to Catholic nationalists with ward boundary changes and register-tampering, was imposed from outside.—think Clinton, Blair, Ahern, Mitchell, the arm-bending High Priests of the Good Friday Agreement, Belfast 1998 . . . They don't. The Assembly is hamstrung by the rule, imported from Belgium, now in similar trouble for the same reason, all parties of two members or more must join the government Executive—all in or all fall down. Think of the White House shared by First President George W. Bush and Deputy First President Barack Obama ;if either quits, the White House closes down.

What to do? No not ethnic cleansing, but, much simpler, parliament-shifting. The Welsh Wizard, (still so remembered) David Lloyd George, Prime Minister of Great Britain and Ireland 1916-1922. was the Genii of The *1920 Better Government of Ireland Act*. Section 8, Paragraph 7, placed the two Irish parliaments in Dublin and Belfast, respectively,—but note the forgotten second comma, after which comes *"or such places as (both parliaments) may respectively determine"*.

Why is it there? It is not hard to imagine the answer. Changing capitals was all in the air and across the furniture around Whitehall as the most important colonies of white settlers, Australia, began to take up decisions they had made before the war but postponed until after it. They would be a federation (1901). To settle the long rivalry between Melbourne and Sydney, they sent an inquiry body around the world to study other solutions and came back with Washington's, in name, Canberra. So the mandarins writing the Irish Act under Lloyd George's discerning nose, some of whom could remember Canada doing much the same thing, must have visualised a similar situation with Belfast and Dublin, so after a cautionary chat (perhaps) with his Cabinet Secretary... the Welsh Wizard

In 1922 the southern leaders split over an independent republic, and devolution resembling Canada, Not until 1998 at Belfast did the South abandon its constitutional claim to the North's territory, but for only so long as its parliament is rigged to share rule with Catholics. It's not working.

An unfettered electoral franchise, a first for Northern Ireland, will allow new ideological parties to form natural coalitions.

Canada, riven by nationalities, religions and two languages, was the second divided state to copy Washington's precedent in 1863. The first was Switzerland,

With even fiercer divisions, calming them ever since the imperial French left in 1848, is tiny neutral capital, Berne. Think—not Sydney, not Melbourne, but Canberra. Not Christian Lagos, not Moslem Kano, but Nigeria, which now struggles to normality since 1992 under brave new neutral capital, Abuja. Does not Irak clearly need three self-governing regions? Would a new capital calm Afghanistan quicker than was tried in three failed centuries of intervening armies? A British phrase for imperial failure dates from the first set-backs in the nineteenth century when her troops were unable to get—*Up the Khyber* . . . to Afghanistan. In the 20th century it was nearly *Up the Falls Road*.

And Israel-Palestine? Split Jerusalem to share as two capitals says Sweden. There is no need. There's lots of room for a new shared neutral site, leaving Jerusalem as Jerusalem for a New Jerusalem. All you need is love, and start with a large marquee for the trial runs. Hebron anyone? Tel Aviv> Ramallah, or just somewhere in between

AND MY PEN PAL BILL

IRISH PARLIAMENT TRUST

Regd Charity 328665 1985-2005

PATRICK J. McGARVEY
DIRECTOR EMERITUS   England

February 9 2010.

Mr. William J. Clinton
President Emeritus
The United State of America

Solutions: Northern Ireland and others.

Dear President Clinton,
 Applauding your work in the peace process, still shaky in Northern Ireland, we suggest it might be finally stabilised by rotating the two premiership posts around all the parties supporting the D'Hondt coalition. Lloyd George's 1920 Better Government Act urged ministers of state in both Irish parliaments to sit and debate in the other when mutual interest arose, but not vote—a forgotten aid to friendship and closer alliances.
 Another idea of ours, this time copied from the substantial Ulster Scots role in the foundation of America (Blythes and Clintons to the fore from the 18th century ships) culminating in the establishment of neutral Washington as capital, let both Irish parliaments share the same space on a neutral site. That too is permitted by the 1920 Act, and copied into the 1937 Irish Constitution

America was copied by:

Switzerland	Berne
Canada	Ottawa
Australia	Canberra
Brazil	Brasilia
Nigeria	Abuja.

Others from Germany to Egypt and Japan simply swapped rival capitals to get the same result; ethnic and religious rivals live in harmony when the center of power is not in either camp. So, why not offer Israel and Palestine the shared sacrifice of neither sharing Jerusalem in favour of a new capital shared by two parliaments.

Try it too on Lebanon, Cyprus, Irak, Kashmir, Indonesia.

All Americans would surely agree that this theme, with such successful precedent, is preferable to sending US troops abroad to fight and die for democracy. America herself has the precedent, and the key. So why not start with the Irish on St. Patrick's Day.

I was on my childhood playground, The Mall, Armagh, when you spoke so movingly to us in September 1998. You were the second great American leader I heard there. The other, in 1944, was General George C. Patton

All Blessings

WILLIAM JEFFERSON CLINTON

March 19, 2010

Patrick J. McGarvey

Dear Patrick:

Thank you very much for taking the time to share your thoughts with me.

It's vital that we discuss the issues that are important to us, and I appreciate your ideas. As I work to improve our world, I'm grateful for your support.

All the best to you.

Sincerely,

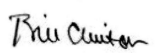

Well Bill, as my first employer, kind, gentle lawyer Vincent Mulholland taught me to write, ***that this indenture witnesseth***, I can only hope your world includes my world. But I also think that one of your successors will come round to our way of thinking, that is, perhaps, President Hillary Clinton. For now, we must be content with the best US Secretary of State since Dean Acheson, hoping that she will pluck the flowers in the Irish constitutions that allow her two parliaments to flourish side by side.

Lightning Source UK Ltd.
Milton Keynes UK
UKOW03f0237080914

238193UK00003B/190/P